One day at a time

Daily Encouragements

Jack Sayers

Copyright © Jack Sayers, 2022

Interior design by Bobby Sayers
Front cover design by Shane and Tom Sayers

Percentage of profits donated to Rethink Mental Illness.

All rights reserved. No part of this publication may be reproduced, stored in a retrieval system, or transmitted, in any form or by any means, electronic, mechanical, photocopying, recording or otherwise, without the prior permission of the author.

I dedicate this book to the following people:

My mentor, Daisaku Ikeda, in whose spirit it was originally written. Thank you for proving with your life the amazing strength, courage and joy we can unleash from within, even during our darkest hours.

My family: I love each and every one of you so much! My biological family, you are all awesome, and a shout out to my lovely in-laws too. Thank you to each of you for your special influence and support in my life and the life of my incredible daughter who I co-parent. My daughter Pippa – you are an incredible human being and will always continue to shape who I am for the better.

Thank you to my family for your proof-reading in the early days and a big shout out to my lovely Mum who was chief proof-reader originally. Thank you so much for your support and comments. Thank you to Elizabeth Hudson for your incredibly professional proof reading thereafter. It profoundly moved the book forward.

Bobby, overall editor and producer. Thanks for all your time, effort and for giving me space to make progress. Tom and Shane – thank you for your support along the way too with thoughts, edits, comments including discussions over the book cover in the early days. And Shane, thanks so much for getting me over the line with your amazing work on the book's cover and final production.

I also want to dedicate this book to an ex-student of mine called Annabelle. I was very fortunate to support and work with you in my role within my school many years ago. I am so pleased I have been able to keep in contact beyond the years to see how life has progressed for you and your family – even having the pleasure of meeting up with you and your family all these years later.

With additional thanks to:

A massive thank you to Rethink Mental Illness, who have so kindly agreed to appear on the front cover so that readers are aware that a percentage of the profits of this book will be given to Rethink Mental Illness.

Thank you also to Kirsty for suggesting that staff at my school be sent the original emails many moons ago, to Bana Gora for your suggestion of two incredible Islamic scholars to include during our wonderful ad hoc conversation at Amsterdam International airport, and to all those at CNS school in Norwich, UK, who have supported me along the way.

And lastly, Dad, we all love you. You have been through so much these past few years. Keep going, and find your happy.

The Author

I'm a co-parent, father, Nichiren Buddhist, teacher, philosopher and all round imperfect person, with ADHD for good measure. I'm not a Google images Buddhist i.e. I don't live in a monastery with my head shaved with a saffron robe. In my Buddhism, and my life, I am working to turn my suffering into causes for future happiness. This is the land, the place, where we find our happiness; each has their own path in life. I'm just another one of the billions of human beings on this beautiful planet spinning around the sun, trying my hardest to enjoy the great moments of life, and to growingly love myself from the inside out so I too can ride the waves of suffering. This idea that joy and hope are more often than not a decision has been reinforced for me, by the life and actions of my mentor Daisaku Ikeda, an incredibly inspiring Buddhist, philosopher and activist for peace, who I have referenced in the dedications section above. The philosophy of Nichiren which I uphold says to us, when the sun is shining let's feel it's warmth glowing radiantly on our skin with deep gratitude, and when dark clouds fill the sky, let us ever move towards the turning point, reaching out for support from those we trust, love and care for. Mr Ikeda has taught me that as we proudly start to climb the often steep path back to happiness, let's create treasured memories as we look back on our many journeys to become happy once again.

I wanted to add here that after I wrote this book I have also encountered the work of Dr Gabor Maté and Richard Swarze. Their works, the works of their contempories, and those they collaborate with and are supported by, have substantially changed my life for the better.

The Book

This book of supportive encouragements is intended to be for everybody who wishes to embrace it. You may take a quick look at today's quote before the rush off to work, after getting the kids ready for school, or together as you begin the day caring for a loved one. It may be that you have a moment longer to consider how the encouragement itself relates to the situation you find yourself in, and my deepest wish is that you feel these words supporting you right there and then, and inspiring you to take hope filled action each day. Whatever situation you may be in, I hope that this book serves as a daily opportunity to realise how significant we all are in this world. I hope that reading the daily encouragements becomes a habit, a short but important moment to yourself, as checking in daily can never be underestimated in a world that often feels stuck on fast forward. I hope deeply that you feel me with you, sharing the struggle, and that you feel as though you are getting to know me more with each passing day, knowing that I too am facing the joys of my life with a smile, and on my darkest days, I too am struggling to find light to brighten my way. I hope my words resonate with you, renewing your determination to make growth from within your circumstances. I will always be touched by the times people have been there for me, encouraged me, and supported me – especially in my most humbling moments. It is my deepest wish that this book allows you to open up and accept the words intended for you. Thank you so much for looking through this book and sharing the year with me; one day at a time.

January 1st

"Let our New Year's resolution be this: we will be there for one another as fellow members of humanity, in the finest sense of the word"

Goran Persson

I imagine you have many reflections on the year gone by; many considerations of what you would like to do differently this year. If you would love to move forward from last year, and every year before in fact, then one important thing is to use any negatives (the manure from last year's decisions) as the fertiliser for your growth in the person you will become this year. This is not a blame game. This is about taking responsibility for our growth, whilst remaining open to others around us; proudly taking the lead in moving forward our relationships with those we will spend our time with this year.

January 2nd

"Happiness can be found even in the darkest of times, if one only remembers to turn on the light"

Albus Dumbledore

The new year can be exciting and invigorating, but all that we are struggling with internally and externally, can often feel overwhelming at this time of year too. Whether today feels beautiful and exciting to you, or it has begun with an internal struggle, please keep looking forward, not back – at what you can do, not what you cannot. This is where the light lies, a light that starts at the centre of you, that shines as you take one step forward at a time.

January 3rd

"The most difficult thing is the decision to act, the rest is merely tenacity. The fears are paper tigers... You can act to change and control your life; and the procedure, the process is its own reward"

Amelia Earhart

I hope that reading this little book lifts your heart a little, gives you that little bit more hope, hope that allows you to move forward in areas of deadlock in your life. No goal or aspiration is too small, and conversely, overwhelming aspirations must begin somewhere. Why not use the new year as that impetus. I wholeheartedly hope you take some step, however small, towards changing something you wish to move forward on today, shaking off the fear of failure to feel the joy of beginning something new in your life.

January 4th

"Don't pray when it rains if you don't pray when the sun shines"

Satchel Paige

As a Brit, I'm no stranger to complaining about difficulties. It is a natural response, as we want to avoid or eliminate the obstacles in our lives. In an ideal world this complaint will lead swiftly to action, to changing our circumstances, or even our attitude towards them. If you are in the midst of suffering I hope you find the inner strength to act to alleviate this for yourself or others. If your obstacles today, however, are small and easily surmountable, I hope you experience a lifting sense of appreciation and gratitude for the positive elements of your life. Whilst having gratitude for the good things is often the last thing we bring to mind, social scientific research shows that doing so regularly can have measurable effects on our wellbeing.

January 5th

"There are no strangers here; Only friends you haven't yet met"

William Butler Yeats

Looking for the potential in others helps us to realise the potential in ourselves. Giving new people the benefit of the doubt, is the difference between closing our life to their potential through ignorance, and expressing compassion towards them, through the realisation of the dignity of each life. Today, I hope that we are truly able to greet the new people we meet with profound respect for their innate potential. If we are truly open to others, we will bring the positive benefit of expanding our sense of self. As we make great efforts to respond to others with genuine respect for them and their views, we cannot help but realise how very special our potential is too.

January 6th

"We have become long on quantity, but short on quality"

Dr Bob. Moorehead

To what extent do our money and material possessions actually make us happy? Studies on wealth and happiness over the last 50 years show that whilst having a sustainable amount of wealth does coincide with happiness levels, as we get money and possessions beyond that which we need, the happiness we gain is short lived. What seems to sustain our happiness is strong relationships, with our friends, our family, loved ones, or our communities, in which we know we can rely on them in times of need. In this light, today, when the opportunity presents itself, let's really be there for that somebody that needs us, and if we require support, let's please reach out with sincerity to ask someone who we can trust to support us today.

January 7th

"The only way to deal with an unfree world is to become so absolutely free that your very existence is an act of rebellion"

Albert Camus

Who is 'the real you' that you sincerely wish to become deep inside? This person, this real you, is a person of integrity, who believes that they can pursue their dreams without fear; a person of hope, who believes that every action we can take for others, does make a real difference to them. So how can we live a life of unsurpassed self-belief and really make a difference, when everyone is telling us it's impossible or telling us our luck is fixed? One step in the right direction is to act from the heart, unmotivated by people's instant reactions. May today be an opportunity to take a step, however small, towards aligning who we are with who we truly want to be.

January 8th

"I hated every minute of training, but I said, 'Don't quit. Suffer now and live the rest of your life as a champion'"

Muhammad Ali

You may be going through a difficult time with work perhaps, or it may be a personal struggle you yourself or a family member is engaged in – one that you are directing great effort towards overcoming. Please never forget that every effort you make towards winning in your goal or aspiration, or to overcome suffering, is benefit that is both intrinsic and extrinsic. No one can take away the self-growth that you gain through your out-and-out struggle to succeed. Please keep going and never give up, whatever difficulties you are facing at present. Please be proud of everything you have done so far in your struggle.

January 9th

"To be yourself in a world that is constantly trying to make you something else is the greatest accomplishment"

Ralph Waldo Emerson

Can we do this in a society where our peers, friends, family, jobs, advertising etc. exert pressure on us to conform to certain norms? Norms such as morality are the glue of our society and they must remain, but a homogeneous culture can damage it, and homogeneous personalities damage it too. Please be yourself today, expressing who you are with great confidence, whilst giving others the space to do the same. Please compare yourself only to who you want to be, not to others, but never judge yourself for not being there yet, for one must not judge the destination whilst one is still on the journey.

January 10th

"It is impossible to live without failing at something, unless you live so cautiously that you might as well not have lived at all, in which case you have failed by default"

J. K. Rowling

Rowling states that it is our choices that we should be judged by, not our abilities. I couldn't agree more. Taking bold steps to be happy, is to develop and grow. The problem with following your heart or aspirations is fear of failure, and overcoming negative doubts that you will have when you are considering taking action. I hope that today you find extra courage (and time) to begin the process of putting your all into achieving your personal and wider goals, so that regardless of the outcome, you do not look back and say, what if?

January 11th

"I'm afraid that if you look at a thing long enough, it loses all of its meaning"

Andy Warhol

Thinking about your purpose often diminishes it, as you go around in circles and circles in your mind. I believe this is because it is impossible to truly understand one's purpose by intellect alone. I could think intellectually about my view that life has meaning when you contribute towards the happiness of oneself and others, until the cows come home, but mere contemplation reduces how special it is to live like this, to a series of words. Living out your life unique to you, in a way that contributes value as you are, is to let the meaning of life pulse through your actions, day by day.

January 12th

"You will find peace not by trying to escape your problems, but by confronting them courageously. You will find peace not in denial, but in victory"

J. Donald Walters

The continual battle we are engaged in to surmount our problems is in itself a victory, as long as we vow to keep on going whatever happens. To pick yourself up each time a problem knocks you back, to work hard to lift yourself each time something brings you down, that is true victory in life. Strength of character is not being unaffected by things, it is keeping going in the face of adversity. This is where the most profound battles to master ourselves are won, and the greatest gains of character are made. Do not give up. Whatever you are facing today, know that by continuing to face struggles, you begin to overcome them.

January 13th

"I follow three rules: Do the right thing, do the best you can, and always show people you care"

Lou Holtz

All three of these rules seem to be backed up by three decades of social scientific research into happiness. Holtz's first rule brings a strong sense of self-worth, his second leads to mindful living; gratitude manifesting itself in action for others, and the final rule is ultimately the premise of both altruism and engagement. So that's all five elements of a happier life that the research reveals (self-worth, mindful living, gratitude, altruism and engagement) backed up by the research. It may be a struggle to apply one of these throughout our day today, let alone all three, but no matter how difficult they are, living a day with these intentions gives a feeling of self-belief in who we can become.

January 14th

"The most beautiful people we have known are those who have known defeat, known suffering, known struggle, known loss, and have found their way out of those depths"

Elisabeth Kübler-Ross

It may be that, as you read this, you, or those close to you are facing profound suffering. Often in the face of this we are incredibly overwhelmed and naturally feel helpless. If there is a small gesture you can make today to alleviate your suffering, or another's, please make it. If you can find the strength within you, help lift others from the depths, even if only slightly, with your words and support. If it is you that is suffering, please believe in your capacity today to create value from your experiences; to learn and grow. If at best we can only change how we or others feel in the situation, let's start to do that today, so that there is some light in the darkness.

January 15th

The wound is the place where the Light enters you"

Jalal ad-Din Muhammad Rumi

That which is the toughest to endure, is that which so often sends us the strongest message. A message of change, a message of action and a message that we need to share our suffering with those we most trust as we begin to look for support and grow. And when we look back, we find that our darkest moments, so often lead to the deepest inner clarity and long term change, given the passage of time.

January 16th

"Each person holds so much power within themselves that needs to be let out... they just need a little nudge, a little direction, a little support, a little coaching, and the greatest things can happen"

Pete Carroll

It so important to realise how incredibly great we can be, the difficulties we can surmount, and the value we can create. It just takes someone to point it out to us in a way that resonates with us. Let's look for opportunities in which we can help other people believe in their abilities, their potential, their capacity for change. Whether it be our family, friends, loved ones, or anybody we interact with; let's be there for them when we can. As their trust in us grows, let's realise that in being there for them we have already nudged ourselves in the right direction too.

January 17th

"If you don't like something, change it. If you can't change it, change your attitude"

Maya Angelou

Civil rights activist Angelou makes an important statement here, which is also echoed by Holocaust survivor and psychologist, Viktor Frankl, who says, "When we are no longer able to change a situation...we are challenged to change ourselves." But is this really possible to do? After facing the deepest of suffering, they say to us "do not walk a path of despair" and, where possible, use this desire for change. To direct this desire to those areas of our lives, and the lives of others, in which we still can create value is to live a truly admirable life of hope and determination.

January 18th

"No matter how closely you examine the water, glucose, and electrolyte salts in the human brain, you can't find the point where these molecules became conscious"

Deepak Chopra

Whilst it makes sense evolutionarily to develop consciousness, the brain's complexity in achieving this, still continues to challenge scientists to this very day. Consciousness is incredible, yet for many of us it can be such a difficult experience. In suffering or regret, our conscious mind can even seem to turn on us, casting a further shadow on an already difficult enough event. Today though, it is my deepest wish that you can truly understand the positives of being in your corner of the universe – a protagonist within the environment you find yourself, able to breathe slowly, and be reminded how special it can be, to be.

January 19th

"Do not be led by others, awaken your own mind, amass your own experience, and decide for yourself your own path"

The Atharva Veda

If you are experiencing success in an area of your life, please keep growing, viewing your current achievements as the causes for future success too. If you are doing well in some area of your life at present, don't stagnate, continue to grow, so that with the next challenge you face, you can use the confidence you gained from the last. If today however is a time of difficulty, failure or regret, use this suffering as the very reason to awaken to your own path as you fight to build your future happiness today.

January 20th

"Life's most persistent and urgent question is, 'What are you doing for others?"

Martin Luther King Jr.

Dr King is absolutely right: there is no true everlasting happiness if we do not fight for and preserve the happiness of those around us too. Concerning ourselves with the happiness of our friends, family, and that person right in front of us, helps us break out of the shell of our ego, our lesser self, which can tend to take over from time to time. It helps us grow beyond our current selves, to become happy when we see happiness in others too. Let's move forward with the aim for our actions to lead to the happiness of others when such opportunities present themselves to us today.

January 21st

"I do believe that if you haven't learnt about sadness, you cannot appreciate happiness"

Nana Mouskouri

Happiness comes because obstacles become one with the triumph we win over them. Therefore, although they are strongly contrary to our initial wellbeing, problems are often necessary to reach our highest state of contentment, for winning over them determinedly and resiliently, we develop a great sense of self-worth. Neuroscience tells us of brain neuroplasticity. This means that as we work hard to break through our difficulties, struggling in the midst of them, we are actually creating new neural pathways in our brain in the process. In short, as we grow as a person, we are growing more able to face the next challenge as an opportunity to become happier.

January 22nd

"I find that if I am thinking too much of my own problems and the fact that at times things are not just like I want them to be, I do not make any progress at all. But if I look around and see what I can do, and then I do it, I move on"

Rosa Parks

Taking a little bit of positive action can be giving a smile to someone we come into contact with, sending a message to someone for whom we care, or doing a favour here or there. If we can do this kind of thing, especially in the midst of our own struggles, we can begin to feel part of something bigger than ourselves. Social scientific research from the last few decades shows us that by making a little difference to those around us we begin to lift the clouds from our own heart too. So let's reach out to others when those little opportunities arise.

"The purpose of life, I believe, when viewed in perspective, is finding a balance between morals and material imperatives. A balance is needed for finding true happiness in life"

Abdurrahman Wahid

Wahid served as the first democratically elected President of Indonesia. As a champion of human rights and religious freedom, he made it his life's effort to promote a sense of social responsibility towards others. If we lack the wisdom to acquire and spend wealth in a way that considers others, then the happiness we ourselves amass will be short-lived. Today, let's act for our material needs whilst considering the balance of what is right in the process. If we can get this balance right, by supporting our lives in ways which bring us integrity, then we continue to grow each day as human beings.

January 24th

"It's not what you look at that matters, it's what you see"

Henry David Thoreau

Our perception of events that unfold in our lives is shaped by our attitude towards them. If we develop the habit over time of seeing the difficulties we face as opportunities to grow, as we bring forth great strength to overcome them, it brings great meaning to our suffering. Meaning in our suffering can be a game changer that allows us to courageously challenge our difficulties head on. Really face your challenges head on today, saying in your mind, "right now I am using great strength to overcome this obstacle", as by admitting that you are growing to meet the problem, you admit that the problem has made you all the stronger for fighting to overcome it.

January 25th

"Our patience will achieve more than our force"

Edmund Burke

Sometimes we need to take direct action to alleviate our suffering or the suffering of others – when we have the wisdom to know what to do, and the courage to do it. There are other times when, regardless of the action we take or the efforts we put in, we cannot seem to change our situation. In such times, Burke is right. Patience or endurance is incredible action in itself, and by having the fighting spirit to keep going, we have already found victory in our attitude. By refusing to give up and be defeated, we prove the inherent greatness of the human spirit, and in doing so we show others that they too possess this inherent greatness. Refuse to give up on your challenges today and you might just see a spark of brilliance inside you: the spark of hope.

January 26th

"Social media is an amazing tool, but it's really the face-to-face interaction that makes a long-term impact"

Felicia Day

Like all areas of technological advance, social media has a mixed impact: it is an incredible platform for freedom of expression, enabling waves of change, creativity and connection, yet some studies have shown that it's over use can have a detrimental impact on our wellbeing, sense of self, and can entrench polarisation. Let us not forget our ability to still send a physical letter, pick up the phone, or even to meet each other, person-to-person, if we can. Let's work to treasure our connection to those we care about through a variety of means.

January 27th

"But there was no need to be ashamed of tears, for tears bore witness that a man had the greatest of courage, the courage to suffer"

Viktor Frankl

As a Holocaust survivor, Frankl bore witness to the most heinous acts of depravity that humanity can stoop to. He suffered in numerous ways: physically, emotionally, losing those he loved, losing his dignity and his health. Through this, one of his messages to us is: "be proud to have the courage to suffer, for your suffering is evidence of your continuing, it is evidence of your true humanity – that you are truly human". If you are facing intense trials at the moment, my deepest prayer is that you find meaning in your suffering, so that it eventually becomes an incredible part of the journey of the person you are to become.

January 28th

"Dare to be happy"

Gertrude Stein

Dare to be happy, dare to challenge the areas of your life that bring you unhappiness. Develop habits that bring happiness to you and others around you, and work towards the acceptance, and eventually the utilisation, of the elements of your life that you cannot change. This is no easy feat - to start challenging our lives in this way today will take real determination. There will be tough times that seem to stop us in our tracks, just when we seem to be on the brink of something special. May they be proof of our progress so far.

January 29th

"By the will art thou lost, by the will art thou found, by the will art thou free, captive, and bound"

Angelus Silesius

Some studies estimate that we can control between 40% to 65% of our happiness; the rest is down to our genes and circumstances, which give us our happiness set point (a general way of feeling about the world). With the realisation that we can take action to improve our long-term happiness, self-fulfilment and improvement are no longer mere coincidence. Let's make concerted long-term efforts for our happiness, and the happiness of others around us, in the confidence that we will grow each day in resilience and strength to face the events outside of our control. Let's begin making this effort to create happiness for our long-term selves today.

January 30th

"Walking with a friend in the dark is better than walking alone in the light"

Helen Keller

Type in Helen Keller into Google and you will soon realise why I am astounded by what an incredible person she was. Her friend in the dark was her teacher, and eventually lifelong companion, Anne Sullivan. Sullivan was blind and Keller deaf-blind. Their incredible relationship meant that they achieved the seemingly impossible together. It shows that if we really stick by each other, are really there for each other, there is no telling how profound an impact we can have. Please be there for others today and reach out to those close to you if you really need their help or an ear.

January 31st

"You've got to stay strong to be strong in tough times"

Tilman J. Fertitta

Just as an athlete has to constantly train to develop her physical muscles, so we too can view our smaller everyday problems as a series of spiritual workouts, so our mindset is shifted, growing in determination, grit, courage and compassion. With this shift in mindset, we can begin to use every ounce of what we find ourselves facing, turning some of life's most challenging difficulties over time into victories – victories in which we grow in character and develop incredible qualities that allow us to improve our lives further. As we face our difficulties today, let's try to continue to view them as challenges to overcome.

February 1st

> "Wherever you are, be there totally. If you find your here and now intolerable and it makes you unhappy, you have three options: remove yourself from the situation, change it, or accept it totally. If you want to take responsibility for your life, you must choose one of those three options, and you must choose now. Then accept the consequences"

Eckhart Tolle

Tolle is asking the most difficult thing of us: to accept responsibility for our circumstances. Accepting responsibility for our circumstances does not mean we are the cause of them; it does not mean that we chose them. Instead it is to believe in our capacity to take hold of where we are right now and create hope there, until things move in the right direction.

February 2nd

"I think we all have blocks between us and the best version of ourselves, whether it's shyness, insecurity, anxiety, whether it's a physical block, and the story of a person overcoming that block to their best self. It's truly inspiring because I think all of us are engaged in that every day"

Tom Hooper

Often our negative view of ourselves overshadows reality. If we learn to bring ourselves quickly from self-judgement towards action, we can change our circumstances for the better. If we can take the determination and courage to do just that, then we begin to creatively use what happens to us to grow. If we can learn to grow with each situation, we turn mistakes into lessons, achievements into self-esteem, and ultimately we grow stronger and happier.

February 3rd

"Words are singularly the most powerful force available to humanity. We can choose to use this force constructively with words of encouragement, or destructively using words of despair. Words have energy and power with the ability to help, to heal, to hinder, to hurt, to harm, to humiliate and to humble"

Yehuda Berg

The words we choose in our interactions today can have a profound effect on us and others. How we speak to other people really can contribute to their wellbeing and happiness. Thus we should feel empowered by how constructive we can be within our immediate environment. We do really make a difference, we really do matter. Never forget that today, when you are truly listening and responding to that person in front of you.

February 4th

"Worry never robs tomorrow of its sorrow, it only saps today of its joy"

Leo Buscaglia

Developing the ability to experience the present moment without complication, is a truly special trick to have up your sleeve, especially when you most need it. Living mindfully can reduce our anxieties, and help with our sleep, as mindfulness means putting worry aside and just experiencing what is actually there in that moment. There is no doubt that this can be incredibly difficult to accomplish in the midst of everyday life, but I sincerely hope that there are a few moments today when you appreciate the truth of what's really going on at work or at home, and rather than judging it, you think of this as encouragement and smile.

February 5th

> "There is no end to education. It is not that you read a book, pass an examination, and finish with education. The whole of life, from the moment you are born to the moment you die, is a process of learning"

Jiddu Krishnamurti

Let's never forget that we are constantly growing and developing our wisdom every day. This understanding is integral to reshaping our self-image. By appreciating that we grow with each problem we face head on, each mistake we learn from, we begin to see how hope and optimism come hand in hand with an ever-changing self. Let's use today as a process of learning – learning from the mistakes we make and feeling positive about next time – rather than dwelling on that which did not go right in a given situation.

February 6th

"Life can only be understood backwards; but it must be lived forwards"

Søren Kierkegaard

I love this concept as it emphasises how precious our lives are, and it also implies that every single day we can make a difference. To know how great life can be, is to have lived at least one day in a creative and contributive way. It is to live in a way that expresses the most special part of being human: the part where we connect with others.

February 7th

"None of us can exist in isolation. Our lives and existence are supported by others in seen and unseen ways, be it by parents, mentors or society at large. To be aware of these connections, to feel appreciation for them, and to strive to give something back to society in a spirit of gratitude is the proper way for human beings to live"

Daisaku Ikeda

In life, regardless of the ups and the downs, I am especially grateful for my treasures of the heart that I have developed along the way, i.e. the connections I have with those around me: my family, my mentor, my friends, and anyone who on a day-to-day basis, contributes to and shares with the ever-changing me. I hope that you have someone in mind that right now that makes you feel gratitude in this way.

February 8th

"As a single footstep will not make a path on the earth, so a single thought will not make a pathway in the mind. To make a deep physical path, we walk again and again. To make a deep mental path, we must think over and over the kind of thoughts we wish to dominate our lives"

Henry David Thoreau

With 100 billion neurons and 100 trillion adaptable pathways connecting these neurons, we cannot doubt the power of our brainsto create new positive psychological response patterns. May this moment, in which we express our gratitude for the positives within our lives, help to retrain and strengthen our pathways to feel a sense of inner strength when we need it the most.

February 9th

"Be kind whenever possible. It is always possible"

The Dalai Lama

We know how great it feels when someone is nice to us, and the great thing is that social scientific research has shown that both the giver of the act of kindness and the receiver of it, benefit from the act itself, even up to four days later. Why not test that today? A lovely, kind little bit of science, in the middle of your day.

February 10th

"Be happy now. Don't wait for something outside of yourself to make you happy in the future. Think how really precious is the time you have to spend, whether it's at work or with your family. Every minute should be enjoyed and savoured"

Earl Nightingale

Social scientific research of the last 20 years has given rise to 5 factors that stand out as contributing to long term happiness and fulfilment, one of which is being mindful in the moment. This is a capability we can develop and improve at any age. Being mindful more often means that we can start to appreciate the little things. Concerning ourselves with the past or future actually causes the opposite so can really interrupt our experience of the here and now. There is no quick fix to feeling happier, but we must never give up on the moments we do feel strong, using them to shape the moments we do not.

February 11th

"If we want to change our world, we do not begin by rectifying the outward. Instead, we must change the condition of our inward"

Hamza Yusuf

If you are going through a tough time please do not give up. Keep smiling when you can, keep positive when you are able to and when you are not able to, never give up, and always have hope in your heart. Continue to reach out for those around you to support you in any way possible and to show you how much they are behind you to keep going, so one day you can look back with pride and say, "I faced that with great courage and eventually I won."

February 12th

"In the long run, the sharpest weapon of all is a kind and gentle spirit"

Anne Frank

How profound and perceptive this incredible young lady was. She is right. The heart of her message is that whilst people are not immortal, the ideals they protect are. If an enduring idea is written into the narrative of history, then the pen is indeed mightier than the sword. The ideas that we write into our lives matter. How we act, what we stand for, matters. It matters to us as the truer we are to what we really believe, the better we sleep at night, and the more comfortable we become living in our own skin. Today, let's live with the fundamental truth of respect for all, as we encounter person after person.

February 13th

"There is in every woman's heart a spark of heavenly fire which lies dormant in the broad daylight of prosperity, but which kindles up and beams and blazes in the dark hour of adversity"

Washington Irving

The one thing that emerges clearly from our adversity, is our strong desire to get out of it; to alleviate our suffering. With a sense of hope in our hearts in our times of difficulty, let's use this fire in our belly, to create value in our situation and become the future example for others in their time of need.

February 14th

"If someone thinks that peace and love are just a cliché that must have been left behind in the 60s, that's a problem. Peace and love are eternal"

John Lennon

I don't claim to be particularly knowledgeable in the area of love but it does seem self-evident that for there to be real love there must be concern, compassion and respect for yourself in equity to that which you grant another. As the Dalai Lama says, "If you don't love yourself, you cannot love others. You will not be able to love others."

February 15th

"One should strongly resent miserliness and indulge in charity because one can acquire the never-ending wealth of immortality by doing so"

The Rig Veda

Really taking an interest and concern in the thoughts, feelings and experiences of others may seem altruistic at the outset, but it pays huges dividends by enriching our own lives. Let's try to treasure at least one person in front of us on this day. Let's see how that feels for them and for us.

February 16th

"This city is what it is because our citizens are what they are"

Plato

As contributive members of our communities, we can help those around us to be happy every day, we do not have to wait for election time, or until a big event occurs that requires our intervention. We have a substantial effect on our immediate environment, as we add to it – through our acts and disposition – each and every day.

February 17th

"If you want to be happy, be"

Leo Tolstoy

How true it is that a big part of happiness is being in the moment as opposed to reflecting on the past, present or future. One aspect of experiencing happiness means to commit to action and be within it. I call this doing 'non-thinking' activities. When we think about it, if we are in the middle of our favourite hobby, or are dancing, water-skiing, abseiling, or perhaps even something more spiritual such as helping out at a homeless shelter, a particular kind of happiness arises. Let's try to be there in whatever we are doing today, and just experience it as it is, letting the future and past, be just that.

February 18th

"If you fell down yesterday, stand up today"

H.G. Wells

However you choose to interpret this quote – making of mistakes, failing to act on your principles etc. – the message is clear. Let's learn from yesterday, using it as fuel to grow as a person today.

February 19th

"What lies behind you and what lies in front of you, pales in comparison to what lies inside of you"

Ralph Waldo Emerson

Many of us find it difficult to live in the present moment. If we find being mindful of the present tough, let's at least make a conscious effort to remind ourselves how incredibly great we can be and how much of our potential there is left to reveal. Please be kind to yourself today, through the ups and downs, for whatever the day will bring, as you have so much to give, and always will.

February 20th

"Everything we do, every thought we've ever had, is produced by the human brain. But exactly how it operates remains one of the biggest unsolved mysteries, and it seems the more we probe its secrets, the more surprises we find"

Neil deGrasse Tyson

An understanding of what consciousness truly is and how it arises, continues to evade scientists, despite an intense amount of research into this area. As more more theories of consciousnes arise, so do just as many questions. I hope that this idea of the mystic nature of our conscious minds, inspires us to feel in the a truly special protagonist in our lives. May we rise above our suffering and take life affirming decisions today with this knowledge.

February 21st

"Happiness is a choice. You can choose to be happy. There's going to be stress in life, but it's your choice whether you let it affect you or not"

Valerie Bertinelli

Whilst this quote is factually inaccurate, as it oversimplifies things, it expresses a profound truth that a growing number of sociologists, psychologists and neuroscientists who are researching happiness are beginning to see emerge. A large body of evidence concurs that happiness is not something you have or do not have, it is connected to a set of habitual psychological responses to conditions we face, that we can gradually train and strengthen over time with the right philosophy and living. Let's live today with hope in our hearts that the truth is that happiness is something we can work at, together.

February 22nd

"Burn worldly love, rub the ashes and make ink of it, make the heart the pen, the intellect the writer, write that which has no end or limit"

Guru Nanak

Let our love, our kindness, be the oil in the lamp of our life. May the positivity and the compassion we can show to the person in front of us, lift us too, giving us an unshakeable view of ourselves. There has been much social scientific evidence that supports the view that in lifting others we genuinely lift ourselves. Let's add to our story today with the ink of bringing hope to others too; may this page in our story and countless others bring us a smile and pride in time to come.

February 23rd

> **"Our uniqueness, our individuality, and our life experience molds us into fascinating beings. I hope we can embrace that. I pray we may all challenge ourselves to delve into the deepest resources of our hearts to cultivate an atmosphere of understanding, acceptance, tolerance, and compassion. We are all in this life together"**

Linda Thompson

What incredible joy we can find in celebrating our differences and standing together triumphantly to rise above ignorance and misunderstanding. Let's greet others today with a belief that both our individualities matter, and that if we engage with deep respect we can learn something even from the person we most disagree with.

February 24th

"Always do what is right. It will gratify half of mankind and astound the other"

Mark Twain

Twain reminds us that it's not just the effect of our actions that matters, it's the effect of the effects; it is this that impacts wider society. Lorenz' butterfly effect suggests that small initial changes can ultimately cause huge differences later on. We could interpret this to mean that the ripples from a positive stone thrown into a sea of negativity may have profound long-term effects. Today, let's ripple a few positive stones in a pond of people waiting and hoping that someone will come along a light up the situation. Let's do it whether we can see the ripples or not.

February 25th

> "You are not here merely to make a living. You are here in order to enable the world to live more amply, with greater vision, with a finer spirit of hope and achievement. You are here to enrich the world, and you impoverish yourself if you forget the errand"

Woodrow Wilson

When we ask each other, "what do you do?", wouldn't it be inspiring if we could have the courage to talk about the difference we make in all areas of our lives, rather than purely give the job title of our employment? Let's strive to create value in whatever we do today, wherever we are, and whoever we are with. For today matters and the people in our day give us the opportunity to spread a little happiness.

February 26th

"It is very important to know who you are. To make decisions. To show who you are"

Malala Yousafzai

Being who we are is no easy feat when we often cannot get to grips with the person we are most comfortable being. When we act sincerely and with our hearts however, we can begin to learn those actions that sit well with us, that feel real, that feel natural. Providing we consider the effects our actions have on others too, pursuing a path of being at ease with that which we do, can support our wellbeing, our lives; particularly through times of turmoil.

February 27th

"A grateful heart is a beginning of greatness. It is an expression of humility. It is a foundation for the development of such virtues as prayer, faith, courage, contentment, happiness, love, and well-being"

James E. Faust

Gratitude is difficult to cultivate, but by no means impossible. Studies have shown that a genuine daily recording of that which one is grateful for makes people happier over time. Whether it is just thinking about what we appreciate in our lives for a minute or so each day or writing it, what we are starting to do is retrain our minds to put a positive spin on things, which over time can completely change our ability to live in each moment, not analyse it. If we think we may have no time to think of something we are deeply grateful for, let's do it now, so we can hold that thought in our hearts today.

February 28th

"Opportunities are usually disguised as hard work, so most people don't recognize them"

Ann Landers

Picture the scene: you've got a problem, a difficulty but then suddenly you have a realisation that actually it's a really tough challenge, but a tough challenge you can slowly overcome. Making this shift may seem trivial but actually it can transform suffering by bringing forth hope, resilience and courage. Never forget that all the adversities you can transform may bring you the greatest of joy.

February 29th

"As societies grow decadent, the language grows decadent, too. Words are used to disguise, not to illuminate, action: you liberate a city by destroying it. Words are to confuse, so that at election time people will solemnly vote against their own interests"

Gore Vidal

We have to be especially vigilant not to be swayed by rhetorical devices used by the media, or those who speak to the people through the media. We must appeal to reason and logic to determine whether arguments being made are strong or not. This coherent approach will help us to avoid our own personal biases and navigate a difficult political landscape. Not only that, it will help us to navigate what is being said to us today, so we can be true to ourselves.

March 1st

"To embrace the whole world in friendship is wisdom. This wisdom is not changeable like the flowers that bloom and fade"

Thiruvalluvar

It's no easy feat to embrace the good side of those who we may find disagreement and conflict with. Their good qualities, however, exist and having the patience to understand that their good qualities are there, deep within – however latent they might seem – can at times be life changing. Showing this deep respect for others demonstrates a sincerity in our communication with them that opens the door to dialogue in times of difference and difficulty. To embrace one another's humanity and each other's good side is what Gandhi refers to when he says, "In a gentle way, you can shake the world." Let's give our world a little shake for the better today.

March 2nd

"Most people want more income and strive for it. Yet as Western societies have got richer, their people have become no happier. This is no old wives' tale. It is a fact proven by many pieces of scientific research. As I'll show we have good ways to measure how happy people are, and all the evidence says that on average people are no happier today than they were fifty years ago, yet at the same time average incomes have more than doubled. This paradox is equally true of the United States, and Britain, and Japan"

Richard Layard

It is not wrong to pursue wealth to a certain extent, but it is definitely incorrect to equate it with happiness in and of itself. After achieving a comfortable standard of living, we need to look to enrich other areas of our lives, whether these be our friendships, family connections, or our ability to positively connect with the person in front of us today.

March 3rd

"The fact that I can plant a seed and it becomes a flower, share a bit of knowledge and it becomes another's, smile at someone and receive a smile in return, are to me continual spiritual exercises"

Leo Buscaglia

It is one of life's joys that we can help others to feel joy. It is the shortcut to feeling truly alive, truly meaningful. If we notice a little opportunity to make someone smile today, to share some words that lift someone's spirit, let's do it and let's feel how truly special it can be to be human in the process.

March 4th

"Hope is being able to see that there is light despite all of the darkness"

Desmond Tutu

What if today we have the realisation that the light in the tunnel is much closer than we think – in fact the light comes from within. It is a light revealed through strength, courage and determination. Let us keep going with the knowledge that this light is deep within us today.

March 5th

"Let him who would move the world first move himself"

Socrates

It is so important that we are not overwhelmed by the difficulty of making a change on the macro level. If we make great efforts to change things in our lives and become truly happier, others will see our example and have the drive to follow. Let us be empowered and enriched by the positive changes that we can enact, never belittling our efforts to bring light to others.

March 6th

"We the people, recognize that we have responsibilities as well as rights; that our destinies are bound together; that a freedom which only asks what's in it for me, a freedom without a commitment to others, a freedom without love or charity or duty or patriotism, is unworthy of our founding ideals"

Barack Obama

As humans, we have a responsibility to others. We therefore need our capacity to socially judge the rightness and wrongness of actions. We are much quicker to make a judgement on what is right and wrong than to make decisions about how we ourselves wish to behave in our own lives. When we do reflect on our behaviour and decide to make a positive impact on our immediate environment, social-scientific research shows that we reduce stress hormones and begin to improve our wellbeing. Let's show sincere care for those around us to test this for ourselves today.

March 7th

"Success in life is founded upon attention to the small things rather than to the large things; to the everyday things nearest to us rather than to the things that are remote and uncommon"

Booker T. Washington

In Confucianism, happiness comes from consistently doing the little things well. Concentrating on the small achievements each day, gaining strength and self-belief as we do, only serves to help us turn obstacles into challenges. This in turn makes us more likely to overcome them and to achieve greater successes in the long run too.

March 8th

"The most authentic thing about us is our capacity to create, to overcome, to endure, to transform, to love and to be greater than our suffering"

Ben Okri

According to Okri, when things are really tough and we persevere with great determination, it is then that we display our truly human attributes; attributes such as courage, wisdom and compassion. Learning to face our day-to-day difficulties head on, acts as a sort of spiritual gym in which we build our inner strength to face life's toughest challenges.

March 9th

"Everyone has inside of him a piece of good news. The good news is that you don't know how great you can be! How much you can love! What you can accomplish! And what your potential is!"

Anne Frank

The most important thing when we realise how much of a positive impact we can make is to put this into practice, even if only for a little while, each day, so that we can emulate this joy for ourselves and others. The important thing is not to doubt how big a difference we can make, but to wholeheartedly enjoy making the difference that we can. I hope we get a chance to enjoy this feeling today.

March 10th

"The highest forms of understanding we can achieve are laughter and human compassion"

Richard Feynman

Winner of the Nobel Prize for Physics for his work on quantum mechanics, Feynman also had great insight into the mechanics of life too. He described the awe and wonder in the quantum world saying, "I think I can safely say that nobody understands quantum mechanics." So whilst we pursue these incredible avenues of how the world works, let us not forget that we already know the most important thing that we will ever discover: the joy of sharing this life with others.

March 11th

"The greatest of all mistakes is to do nothing because you think you can only do a little"

Zig Ziglar

Please never underestimate the difference that the little things you do makes. By considering how much of a difference we can make, today, tomorrow and beyond, we begin to take the initiative to do just that, to believe we can, and to be empowered in the process. Let's live today, with the view that our actions do make a difference.

March 12th

"Consult not your fears but your hopes and your dreams. Think not about your frustrations, but about your unfulfilled potential. Concern yourself not with what you tried and failed in, but with what it is still possible for you to do"

Pope John XXIII

It is so important to base our happiness on our own potential and the potential of the moment. In science, everything is impermanent on a subatomic level. Everything is changing moment by moment in the universe, thus we too by extension are always changing and are always in a state of growing potential, or ever changing possibilties. In Japan there is a phrase 'honin myo' which essentially translates as 'from this moment on'. What matters is what you decide to do from this moment on, for in this moment lies your boundless potential as a human being.

March 13th

"We are constituted so that simple acts of kindness, such as giving to charity or expressing gratitude, have a positive effect on our long-term moods. The key to the happy life, it seems, is the good life: a life with sustained relationships, challenging work, and connections to community"

Paul Bloom

From the science of positive psychology, numerous studies tell us if we connect with others deeply we're much more likely to be happy. In one Harvard study, over a 75 year period they followed over 400 men, interviewing them every two years. The study concluded that those in relationships where they could really rely on others, came out as the most happy, regardless of income. Those who developed strong relationships with either family, spouses, friends or the community, improved their health and life expectancy.

March 14th

"Darkness cannot drive out darkness; only light can do that. Hate cannot drive out hate; only love can do that"

Martin Luther King Jr.

This is one of my favourite quotes of all time for it shows us what each of us should pursue in our own lives. Let's build our happiness from the ground up. Let's start with where we are, with what we have, and create a little light to shine on our circumstances. We can do no more or less than show kindness, caring and decency towards the people we come into contact with today. Let's never forget the incredibly positive but unseen impact we can have on those around us, when we decide whatever happens that we ourselves will light a lamp of hope in the hearts of others.

March 15th

"The purpose of human life is to serve, and to show compassion and the will to help others"

Albert Schweitzer

One of the many meanings we find in our lives can be found in doing our very best to lift ourselves and others around wherever opportunity affords us the chance to do so. By doing the things we are already doing to the best of our ability we will begin to open up our lives to the opportunity to connect with others.

March 16th

"He who is not contented with what he has, would not be contented with what he would like to have"

Socrates

Through the work of Plato, Socrates argues that we must find gratitude in that which we already have in our lives before our pursuit of that which we do not. This could be seen the middle way to self-love; loving who we are and what we have, helping us to love, progress, grow and become the people we wish to be.

March 17th

"Success is not a destination, but the road that you're on. Being successful means that you're working hard and walking your walk every day. You can only live your dream by working hard towards it. That's living your dream"

Marlon Wayans

As Wayans says, working towards our dream is part of the dream itself. Why? Because working towards our aspirations is inseparable from them; the dream achieved, is the dream worked towards. Perhaps with this firmly in mind we can start to appreciate the hard work we are putting in every day in our lives and begin to see our path to greater fulfilment, as a treasure itself.

March 18th

"Do your little bit of good where you are; it's those little bits of good put together that overwhelm the world"

Desmond Tutu

There is so much good in the world and yet so much evil too. If we do our little bit of good where we are right now, we can gain great pride about which side we are on, which side we are contributing to. Taking the time to show kindness, to listen, to care, really does have an unimaginably profound butterfly effect that we can be proud to be a part of.

March 19th

"Kind words can be short and easy to speak, but their echoes are truly endless"

Mother Teresa

Our greatness is deeply connected to our capacity to lift others. Please remember that importantly, the echo of positivity of these kind words resounds in the heart of those who utter them too.

March 20th

"The years teach much which the days never know"

Ralph Waldo Emerson

Let us continue to strive in our daily interactions with others to develop great friendships, providing support to others around us that will blossom and flower in the years to come. In concentrating on today, we learn about ourselves and our capacity in engender positive change in our immediate environment, contributing to the future we create.

March 21st

"Before comparing yourself with others, win the battle with yourself. Strive to be better today than yesterday, and better tomorrow than today"

Daisaku Ikeda

In my youth I read a book called Social Anxiety, by Alain De Botten, which details the issue of material and social comparison. As well as creating a societal facade that damages the bandwidth of our personal connections, gaining happiness by comparison with others is extremely short-term in it's gain, leading to emptiness again and again. More than this though, comparison with others will make us feel inferior, or superior and neither of these are healthy for our long-term wellbeing. Thus, unique as we are, let's continue on our own personal journey of growth, and let's support others as they too embark on the spiritual quest.

March 22nd

"Great work requires great and persistent effort for a long time. Character has to be established through a thousand stumbles"

Swami Vivekananda

One key component of achieving our most difficult goals is, somewhat unfortunately, arduous and persistent effort. This is something that few of us attain naturally. One important character trait we need to develop is to be able to pick ourselves up every time we drop back, or find ourselves slacking in resolve. It is not falling or failing that matters, it is a failure to get back up, however long it takes. If we vow to keep going each time we are off track, and, forgiving ourselves, vow to encourage ourselves to push forward once again, we cannot but win for we have already won in our hearts.

March 23rd

"It is better to light one small candle than to curse the darkness"

Confucius

Whatever is happening on a macro level, we have the capacity to make a difference right now, within our friendship groups, our families, our fellow colleagues/students, and in our local community. When I lived in Norwich, years ago, a leaflet came through my door inviting everyone down our road to join a litter clean-up. The gentleman behind this action was clearly lighting a candle in his local community, and, after contacting him, I joined others in solidarity for the community clean-up. While negativity makes the international news, it is clear that we can all work together to build bridges of friendship which enact a positive change in our immediate environment, whether it be where we work, study or live.

March 24th

"The best way to find yourself is to lose yourself in the service of others"

Mahatma Gandhi

Altruistic behaviour emerges as one the strongest causes of long-term human happiness, when studied in the field of positive psychology. Altruism should go in line with our own happiness and thus not be overdone to the detriment of our own needs or our sense of self. Healthy altruism that allows us to still be who we are, can give us the greatest sense of fulfilment, as we express our true humanity and experience that of others.

March 25th

"Inspiration exists, but it has to find you working"

Pablo Picasso

Picasso is making the case for work first, inspiration later. If we wait for the 'right idea', the 'right solution', there are moments of impasse in which we may wait a very long time. If we get to work on what we can do right now, and do it to the best of our ability, we will find that inspiration, and options, arrive later in the midst of our ardent activity without necessarily realising that we have got there.

March 26th

"Everything can be taken from a man or a woman but one thing: the last of human freedoms to choose one's attitude in any given set of circumstances, to choose one's own way"

Viktor Frankl

In his book, 'Man's Search for Meaning', Psychiatrist and survivor of The Holocaust, Viktor Frankl, demonstrates that when we don't know what to do in a situation, by choosing to carry on, we actually assert our remaining freedom, freedom of the attitude; a freedom that allows us to find meaning in suffering. This freedom, he says, no one can take away from us. His is a story of hope and it is from hope that we begin to face adversity and grow in strength.

March 27th

"As soon as you trust yourself, you will know how to live"

Johann Wolfgang von Goethe

A number of inspirational quotes allude to this idea of aligning who we truly are with how we choose to live our lives. If we can trust ourselves to be the person we want to be, if we can live true to our values and core beliefs, then we will find great fulfilment in becoming the best we can be. Today, tomorrow and beyond.

March 28th

"There is nothing noble in being superior to your fellow man; true nobility is being superior to your former self"

Ernest Hemingway

Comparison with others brings no true joy. Either one is exalted by superiority, disparaging others in the process, or one sees oneself as inferior, which denies our inherent and latent dignity. Of course the reality is that neither is true, as all human beings are equal on a profound level; as we all have the potential to shine. So as to not stagnate, we must make efforts to grow beautifully but organically from the person we were one hour, day or month ago, yet paradoxically at the same time, be proud to be who we are, for we are human after all.

March 29th

"Failure is an event not a person"

Zig Ziglar

How much more progress would we make on our own personal journeys if we continued to realise that our short-term setbacks are genuine opportunities to learn and grow? Escaping the trap of dwelling on these setbacks, or blaming ourselves, we should instead direct all that energy towards positive action and growth; now that is a habit for happiness worth working towards.

March 30th

"He is not strong and powerful who throweth people down; but he is strong who witholdeth himself from anger"

The Prophet Muhammad (pbuh)

Being passive is to stagnate one's character, but being a pacifist in our own lives is in no way lacking in courage. Just because one's anger is not outwardly visible, it does not mean that it is not used to address the injustice and ills of workplace, community, or society at large. One only has to look at great examples from history of outstanding figures who did not raise their fists to enact change. Consider not only the leaders who have achieved fame, but every person who stood with them in solidarity and said 'no' to the circumstances with assertive strength in the midst of the struggle to create a new path.

March 31st

"Happiness is the meaning and the purpose of life, the whole aim and end of human existence"

Aristotle

Clearly we want to be happy, but what does that mean in reality? Some say happiness adorns those who, far from being defeated by life's harshest storms, use them to grow in strength and contribute positively to the lives of others. Others say it is to synthesise one's actions with what one actually believes in one's heart; thus to synthesise the two. There are so many views on happiness but in the science of happiness, which evolved from positive psychology, one common theme emerges. To be truly happy, we have to establish a purpose in our lives, linking the way we live towards aims greater than just ourselves.

April 1st

"Peace cannot be kept by force; it can only be achieved by understanding"

Albert Einstein

We are agents of action within families, communities and societies. If we want to get along with each other, we need to understand the thoughts and feelings of those who we disagree with: what makes them tick, why they think, feel, act as they do, their needs, their position of interest. When it comes to our peace of mind, we often find this is completely out of kilter. Whatever strategy we need to employ to reach inner peace, we often need to first find an understanding of how we came to be unhappy. This understanding can lead to acceptance, and acceptance can lead to beginning again; to working towards the happiness of ourselves and others, once more.

April 2nd

"One who gains strength by overcoming obstacles possesses the only strength which can overcome adversity"

Albert Schweitzer

There are many derivations of the two Chinese characters that make up the word crisis; in one translation of these characters we can see an expression of 'danger' in the first and 'opportunity' in the second. To live a life in which we see our difficulties at the very time when we have a precarious, but important, moment of opportunity to develop our courage and compassion, is to turn such poison into medicine.

April 3rd

"Some people regard discipline as a chore. For me, it is a kind of order that sets me free to fly"

Julie Andrews

What is true liberation of the self? It is to discipline oneself to become what one wants to be. It is to be wholly in charge of one's life, growing in courage and self-belief, as we overcome our obstacles and achieve our goals, one by one. Whilst we strive for this goal of being in charge of our lives fully, we must also accept, appreciate and affirm our humanity in our failure to achieve this all the time. It is then an exciting aspect of ourselves to grow and develop. We should not berate and belittle ourselves when we fall short of this aim, as we are, after all, only human.

April 4th

"I set out to find flawed men and couldn't find any, when I finally peered inside myself though, there was nobody more flawed than me"

Sant Kabir

Happiness is often a matter of hard – fought victory over self-doubt. Doubt that we ourselves are worthy of great respect. Doubt that we will be able to overcome a particular difficulty or obstacle. Doubt that we can ride this particular storm that life has thrown at us. By never giving up on ourselves and others, we begin to allow the sun of hope and courage to rise in our hearts, and thus we grow in strength as we begin the fight to win over our negative tendencies.

April 5th

"We cannot do great things on this Earth, only small things with great love"

Mother Teresa

Far from underestimating the small things we do each day for others, we should remember that the positive contribution we bring to those around us is, in itself, profound. Let's not forget how special we, too, are today. Let's not underestimate our actions on this day, and instead consider the effect that they have on those around us.

April 6th

"Love is what we are born with. Fear is what we have learned here. The spiritual journey is the unlearning of fear and the acceptance of love back into our hearts"

Marianne Williamson

When we consider how equally we are born and how any inequality and hatred are learnt behaviours, it becomes only natural to realise that the true reality of our lives is that each of us should treat one another with the dignity inherent in each of our lives at birth. If most people realised this and were brave enough to live it, we would have peace. Please start today by realising your own unique dignity. Regardless of your thoughts, actions, deeds, please know that you, by your very nature, have an incredible dignity that you were born with. I hope today you can feel, deep down, how very special you are.

April 7th

"You gain strength, courage and confidence by every experience in which you really stop to look fear in the face.... You must do the thing you think you cannot do"

Eleanor Roosevelt

One important aspect of our lives is that the bigger a challenge we face, the more we have to elevate our character to rise to meet it. Thus, facing our challenges head-on develops our character, as we bring out the inner strength and courage needed to succeed. It is in this process we forge a stronger self and experience an elevated existence through the faith that we have the ability to dig deep and create value in the face of adversity.

April 8th

> "Technology can be our best friend, and technology can also be the biggest party pooper of our lives. It interrupts our own story, interrupts our ability to have a thought or a daydream, to imagine something wonderful, because we're too busy bridging the walk from the cafeteria back to the office on the cell phone"
>
> Steven Spielberg

Technology is incredible – medical advances are saving and changing lives and all sorts of new opportunities are at our fingertips. Used correctly, technology can be simply amazing. However, as Spielberg suggests, technology also has the propensity to be overused in daily life and thus interrupt our imaginative processes and ability to interact face to face with people. True face-to-face, heart-to-heart dialogue is what truly creates trust, friendship and peace. From this day on, let's use technology to complement, and never prevent us from seeing the opportunities for happiness that exist right in front of us.

April 9th

"I exist as I am, that is enough, If no other in the world be aware I sit content, And if each and all be aware I sit content"

Walt Whitman

Whitman enables me to reflect on the joy of just being – a joy that we can experience in moments of tranquillity. Working towards a life state when we can access this same level of self-acceptance and tranquillity too, in the face of day to day difficulties, is incredibly hard indeed. It is important at times to take a step back from our difficulties, in order to see ourselves there beyond and behind our suffering. Today, let's take a moment to be, to feel, to breathe, to take sanctuary in the self. For beyond our daily struggles we are special, we are important and we matter. Keep going today. Believe in youself.

April 10th

"Life and death, joy and sorrow, gain and loss; These dualities cannot be avoided. Learn to accept what you cannot change"

The Yajur Veda

Whilst this may seem like an impossible task at times, there are many points in life when we will inevitably experience pain, sorrow or a setback. However, with each setback comes the opportunity though for courage and growth. If we can galvanise just enough courage to push on, we can resolutely begin to turn the poison of our situation into the medicine needed for our growth in overcoming it. Let's take steps today to use our adversity to fuel our advance in achieving great happiness.

April 11th

"Insanity is doing the same thing over and over again and expecting different results"

Albert Einstein

If we feel deadlocked in a particular situation today, approaching it in a completely different way, from a completely different angle or perceiving it with a change in our mindset, can sometimes be just what is needed to kick-start the process of change. Sometimes when we don't know what to do, it is important to do something. It may be something that completely allows us to begin our ascent up a ladder with faith in our first step.

April 12th

"Happiness is not a life without worries or struggles. Happiness is the robust sense of fulfilment one feels when bravely confronting hardship. It is that elevation of the spirit, like an airplane gaining lift from the air resistance against its wings"

Daisaku Ikeda

Please remember that happiness is not the absence of problems, it really is the overcoming of them. Be proud of every struggle and difficulty you have overcome and won in your life so far. We cannot escape suffering and difficulty – unfortunately it is part of life and intrinsic to our personal growth. We can, however, face our problems head-on, and if the difficulties themselves won't shift, then, by not giving up, we will begin to shift our attitude towards the obstacle, so that we can start creating value for ourselves and others exactly as we are.

April 13th

"One can choose to go back toward safety or forward toward growth. Growth must be chosen again and again; fear must be overcome again and again"

Abraham H. Maslow

True happiness is ours through grit – by not shying away from our circumstances day by day, but getting stuck in and winning again and again in different areas of our lives. By retreating from our problems as if they are not there, we go toward safety, but, as we all know, it is a safety that holds out for little time. When Maslow talks about us growing as people and overcoming fear, he means we can adopt the courage of a lion and take on our problems, using them as a source for our growth. Let's advance with this courage today.

April 14th

"Ever tried. Ever failed. No matter. Try Again. Fail again. Fail better"

Samuel Beckett

This is a clear appeal to the argument that never giving up is winning in itself. Let's remember this deep understanding that winning is continuing, winning is carrying on, and winning is learning from our mistakes for the next time. Winning, then, is a state of mind. Let us adopt such a belief today and may our misgivings shape our character for the better, and our difficulties forge us like iron.

April 15th

"Live as if you were living a second time, and as though you had acted wrongly the first time"

Viktor Frankl

Neurologist, psychiatrist and holocaust survivor Viktor Frankl used his experiences to find rich meaning in his life and in doing so he realised how precious and irreplaceable life is. What I love about his quote above is that to genuinely think like this is to really appreciate this chance at life, to really make what we do count. Many people say we should live each day like it's our last, but this is very misleading as it presents us with purely short-term insight. The quote above, however, profoundly sums up how to minimise regret and also have true gratitude for all that we have, and all that we are.

April 16th

"We need more light about each other. Light creates understanding, understanding creates love, love creates patience, and patience creates unity"

Malcolm X

After returning from the hajj, Malcolm X came to understand a life-changing truth that he was unable to then fully enact due to his assassination shortly after. The truth is this: having the patience to understand why others think and feel as they do, is the key to the door of peace. Let's open that door in our own lives today.

April 17th

"As I grow older, I pay less attention to what men say. I just watch what they do"

Andrew Carnegie

This is a great insight from Carnegie that we can take into our day. How we live our lives in our actions, is even more important than the words we utter. Are we taking actions that are bringing a smile to others around us and lifting the spirits of those we come into contact with? Or do we complain or praise the actions of others in the background? We are the protagonists of our day, today. Let's use this opportunity by acting in a way that benefits ourselves and others today, regardless of any of our yesterdays.

April 18th

"For to be free is not merely to cast off one's chains, but to live in a way that respects and enhances the freedom of others"

Nelson Mandela

Our true greatness is connected to our inherent ability to be compassionate in our actions towards those in our immediate vicinity. To have an impact on the happiness of others around us, we must first adopt the belief that we can, and then put this faith in ourselves into solid action organically and naturally, where we are and as we are. The more we naturally support the freedom and happiness of others who we encounter today, the more we realise who we can be.

April 19th

"Remember that not getting what you want is sometimes a wonderful stroke of luck"

The Dalai Lama

There is a beautiful story of the Chinese farmer, which Alan Watts retells. Numerous 'bad fortunes' occur to the farmer, but the constant twist is that things work out for the better in the long run. I'm sure we've all had this experience before. It is important to remember that when things don't go our way in day to day scenarios, this may actually play into our hands in the long run. Especially if we can learn to mould our fate from the situation and our reaction to it. With this hope and optimism, let's use the twists of our tale as fuel for our long-term happiness and victory. Starting from today.

April 20th

"If I am not for myself, who is for me? When I am for myself, what am I? If not now, when?"

Rabbi Hillel

What is Rabbi Hillel really saying to us? I think he means this: if we want to create a better world, let's not hesitate to do so. Let's believe in ourselves. Let's believe in the moment we are in too. We can begin by showing compassion and kindness to those we come into contact with each day. If we do so, we have already embodied peace itself. By doing this, we will not only create positive ripple effects that travel into the future, and which we cannot imagine, but we will also create peace in our own hearts and the hearts of others around us, right here, as we are.

April 21st

"Think of all the beauty still left around you and be happy"

Anne Frank

This is the most important realisation and yet it is often so difficult to achieve – especially when we are suffering. We can make efforts to enable a sense of gratitude to arise in our hearts through habitual reflection. One of my lovely friends gave me a gratitude journal. You simply jot one line down at the end of each day to describe something that you are grateful for, either in general or on that day in particular. Perhaps if we have a moment right now, we could think of one thing about our lives that is of great importance to us, and just for a second imagine our lives without that important element. What would our lives be like? How much harder would they be? These important elements are in our lives already, and a daily realisation of this kind is a small, but substantial, way to move towards growth and acceptance.

April 22nd

"I long to accomplish a great and noble task; but it is my chief duty to accomplish small tasks as if they were great and noble"

Helen Keller

Helen Keller is just one of many scholars who points to proficiency in the smaller things we do. To really live in this way today, to strive to do so, is to appreciate that even the small things we do make a difference to our lives, and the lives others. If we can consistently apply our efforts in this way to the task in front of us, even if these smaller tasks seem somewhat unimportant at the time, we will – as a matter of habit – spend more time in the present, growing to face the evermore demanding moments that life asks of us.

April 23rd

"Ability is what you're capable of doing. Motivation determines what you do. Attitude determines how well you do it"

Lou Holtz

A Japanese conceptual framework devised to help us achieve our potential is kyo chi gyo i. Kyo is the goal you wish to achieve. Chi is the wisdom needed to reach that goal. Gyo is the action you need to take to reach the goal. I (pronounced ee) is the status you will attain when the goal is reached. The key is to proceed in our planning process in this order and focus on the gyo needed for each kyo. By focusing on our gyo we will develop the chi needed to proceed. Too often we focus on i, thus missing out on what we can do right now: moving from the present moment to a future yet to be.

April 24th

"Everyone wants to be appreciated, so if you appreciate someone, don't keep it a secret"

Mary Kay Ash

Sincere appreciation for the ones we love and care for can take the form of that phone call we keep meaning to make, or that letter we have been thinking of writing, or even an email or electronic communication. The key is sincerity. By showing that we care with genuine warmth and compassion, we start to feel gratitude for the other person in our life, and also realise the special capacity we have to make a difference to the lives of others.

April 25th

"All who would win joy, must share it; happiness was born a twin"

Lord Byron

This quote refers to the inseparable nature of happiness for oneself and others. The Japanese term nini-funi – or funi, for short – means "two but not two". Applied to value creation, it means that our actions which bring happiness to others, and those that bring happiness to ourselves, are paradoxically one and the same. When we help others to be happy – genuinely, sincerely and not to our detriment – numerous journals and studies show that we become happier as a result. Excitingly, it is also true that when we take action to improve our situation, and become happier in the midst of difficulty, we show others that they can do it too. Without giving too much of ourselves, let's spread a little happiness today, and keep going in our struggles to inspire others.

April 26th

"Outstanding people have one thing in common: an absolute sense of mission"

Zig Ziglar

One key to being empowered within our lives is to have an overarching mission or purpose that operates subconsciously in the background behind the various elements of who we are and what we choose to do. It can be some aspect of the world we want to be part of, or contribute too. Although it can be anything at all linking to the way we live our lives, it could be linked to the environment, or animal welfare, or the happiness of children, or mental health awareness, or standing up for the rights of others. We don't have to have a mission per se, but formulating values that we are happy to be connected to can really give our life worth and meaning, as we can begin to align our actions with what we want to see improve in the world, and so feel more at ease in being our true selves.

April 27th

"One of the most common causes of failure is the habit of quitting when one is overtaken by temporary defeat"

Napoleon Hill

Our ability to pick ourselves up each time we have a setback is a success in itself, because everyone has setbacks in whatever endeavour they set out to achieve. The best thing to do with our setbacks is to hang on in there, learn and grow. Today we can choose to move forward with strength and belief in positive change, based on the profound insight that arises from our mistakes, difficulties or obstacles.

April 28th

"If you light a lantern for another you brighten your own way"

Nichiren Daishonin

Let's light the way others by not giving up in the face of difficulty. By carrying on and galvanising inner strength to take one small step at a time until we can find happiness again. Let's shine as we are, being true to who we are.

April 29th

"Identify your problems but give your power and energy to solutions"

Anthony Robbins

Initially, dwelling on problems puts them at our heart so that we have clarity about what we want to change. After a while, though, focusing on how we feel about our problems is time that could be spent making a difference to them by coming up with actions that could move things in a positive direction and make us and others feel happier. It sometimes takes great courage to implement such actions. It takes a lot of energy and wisdom to face difficulty head-on, so the less energy we use on dwelling on the suffering itself, the more quickly we rise up and make positive changes with all our being.

April 30th

"You cannot hope to build a better world without improving the individuals. To that end, each of us must work for his [or her] own improvement and, at the same time, share a general responsibility for all humanity, our particular duty being to aid those to whom we think we can be most useful"

Marie Curie

The phrase that beautifully illustrates this journey of self-transformation that Curie is alluding to is, 'human revolution'. Human revolution is the process of overcoming our difficulties by becoming the best version of ourselves we can be. As Curie says, in order to attain our own transformation we must 'share a general responsibility for all humanity' so that we begin to feel connected to – and part of – humanity.

May 1st

"It doesn't matter if you're the smartest person in the room: If you're not someone who people want to be around, you won't get far. Likewise for helping those in line behind you… I make sure my time is tithed"

Melissa Rosenberg

Rosenberg alludes to the inherent truth that to succeed in life is not to succeed over those around you – it is instead to support those around you to succeed too. When you win, I win too; when I win over my struggle, we win together. This works in all spheres, from families, to study, to business, and even to nations. If we share a common bond, we cannot help but want everyone to become happy together. True happiness comes when our growth is built, day by day, in a way that enables others around us to grow too.

May 2nd

"Our uniqueness, our individuality, and our life experience moulds us into fascinating beings. I hope we can embrace that. I pray we may all challenge ourselves to delve into the deepest resources of our hearts to cultivate an atmosphere of understanding, acceptance, tolerance, and compassion. We are all in this life together"

Linda Thompson

Deep within us all is an understanding that all life is dignified, but this is often obscured by personal or group interest. The variety of negative and positive experiences that we have each day should remind us that we are truly human, and that we thus share this humanity with others. Let's take this first step together and go from our egoic self being in the driving seat towards a deep humanist understanding of those around us today.

May 3rd

"Knowledge is power. Information is liberating. Education is the premise of progress, in every society, in every family"

Kofi Annan

Education is a right, but when we look to the availability of it's provision around the world we know too that it is a sincere privilege. It is a privilege that continues throughout our lives, way beyond the days of our formal education. It is a privilege because whatever we learn and however we learn it, whether it be by reading, podcast, streaming, or any other means, it contributes to our growth as human beings, and gives us the tools to raise our spirits and the spirits of those around us.

May 4th

"Many persons have a wrong idea of what constitutes true happiness. It is not attained through self-gratification but through fidelity to a worthy purpose"

Helen Keller

The story of Helen Keller, who fought incredibly hard – together with her lifelong teacher Anne Sullivan – to become the first blind-deaf person to achieve a university degree, is an exceptional story of winning against adversity. Later, as a political activist, she stood up for disability rights, women's rights, and the poor, in addition to defending the philosophy of pacifism. She is an incredible example of how living our life, aligned to ideals and beliefs greater than just ourselves, is one way to work towards a level of happiness we never knew possible.

May 5th

"We don't develop courage by being happy every day. We develop it by surviving difficult times and challenging adversity"

Barbara De Angelis

Courage is an incredible sense of inner strength that often arises when problems and difficulties seem insurmountable. As courage starts to grow, we begin to face our difficulties head on and in doing so, we start to create the best value we can for ourselves and others. In adversity we can become the light within a situation and inspire others so that they too can shine such light. Let's believe in ourselves today, as we slowly grow in courage through facing up to our problems.

May 6th

"Peace begins with a smile"

Mother Teresa

Lorenz' chaos theory shows us, if we take the butterfly effect as a metaphor, that we really do not understand the incredibly profound impact that one smile to one person today could have on the world in the future. All that is required is enough time for the full chain of effects to play out. So let's do it. Let's smile today when we see others, and if possible, give them some parting words of sincerity and compassion. On reflection, after taking such action, we realise how special we and they are, and that we are very connected.

May 7th

"You may not always have a comfortable life and you will not always be able to solve all of the world's problems at once but don't ever underestimate the importance you can have because history has shown us that courage can be contagious and hope can take on a life of its own"

Michelle Obama

We have to be empowered by the difference we do make and never denigrate it as insignificant. In the popular story of the boy who throws back a starfish into the water, on a beach where thousands have unfortunately been washed up by the tide, a man calling from the promenade dissents, "What's the point? You'll never save them all!" As the boy throws the second starfish back in the water he replies, "I've saved this one". If even a small number of us continue to maintain this attitude we cannot help but change the world.

May 8th

"The only way to have a friend is to be one"

Ralph Waldo Emerson

The impact we can have on others is truly profound, and we must never forget that in taking a little time to really be there for our friends, this care and sincerity will be returned to us. If we are strong today, let's be there for others, and if we are struggling, let's reach out to those we trust and be ready to return this love and support to them, when the time comes.

May 9th

"Every day brings new choices"

Martha Beck

By virtue of the infinite possibilities that today brings, we find little strength in dwelling on the negative choices of our past. Today is the day we move forward, a day we begin to change in any way we wish. We may have regrets, the key is that we let them function positively, letting them galvanise us into positive action today, to move the situation forward.

May 10th

"Someone is sitting in the shade today because someone planted a tree a long time ago"

Warren Buffett

This quote reminds me that even if I do not see the positive effects of my actions, by virtue of their ripple effects, there is a very real and tangible difference we can make to others given the passage of time. In a lecture on creating peace one person at a time that I once attended, an individual expressed their feeling of being powerless to enact change. I imagined in my heart a group of incredibly capable and special women just over one hundred years ago, who had every right to express that same feeling of powerlessness whilst campaigning for their suffrage. Although many may not have been able to see the fruits of their efforts, and whilst there is still so far to go for women's equality, this incredible group who never gave up still echo through history. Let's believe in the effects of our actions, and their results yet to come.

May 11th

"Don't watch the clock; do what it does. Keep going"

Sam Levenson

Essentially, our happiness is built on action. There are times when we don't know what to do or are stuck at an impasse, and it is at such times that it is important to take action that creates value for ourselves and others, however limited we feel that may be. It is from this attitude, this intent to keep going, that we begin to sow the seeds that transform our negativity, so that we can begin to face our difficulties with the wisdom, courage and compassion they demand.

May 12th

"Be a rainbow in someone's cloud"

Maya Angelou

I love this quote as it alludes to the fact that as human beings we cannot help but be lifted ourselves when we lift others. Scientific research on wellbeing is confirming more and more that if we expand our lives to really help others around us to be happy, alongside ensuring our own needs are met, we cannot fail to be happier ourselves. As Nichiren Daishonin, the 13th century Buddhist reformer, says, "If you light a lantern for another, it will also brighten your own way." Let's keep an eye out for such opportunities in the midst of our day, today.

May 13th

"Laughter is the sun that drives winter from the human face"

Victor Hugo

Someone very important in my life once said, "if someone is hungry, give them food and if you have no food to give them then at least nourish them with your words. To everyone, give something." The truth of the matter is that laughter by itself is not what gets us through difficult times, but it does relight our humanity and shines a light on the joy ever attainable in our hearts beyond it all. Let's use humour to successfully light our day today.

May 14th

"Courage is the most important of all the virtues, because without courage you can't practice any other virtue consistently. You can practice any virtue erratically, but nothing consistently without courage"

Maya Angelou

Courage is not the absence of fear, it's the overcoming of it, as Nelson Mandela asserts. Courage is staying steadfast to what we believe regardless of the hardships we face and picking ourselves back up with each obstacle or difficulty that knocks us down. In short, it is to continue undaunted by adversity until we can eventually learn to declare that we are happy regardless of these obstacles, and be proud of our personal growth with each obstacle we've overcome.

May 15th

"Logic will get you from A to B. Imagination will take you everywhere"

Albert Einstein

How many times have you been stuck going around in circles in your own head? How true is it that sometimes thinking things through in your own head only gets you so far? In fact, decisions and difficulties that relate to matters of the heart can become entangled in a logic that can't break through. Sometimes by letting go, by beginning to feel our way through with our intuition, our imagination, a way through the deadlock arrives and we begin to take the steps required to create light in darkness.

May 16th

"Every great dream begins with a dreamer. Always remember, you have within you the strength, the patience, and the passion to reach for the stars to change the world"

Harriet Tubman

Tubman incredibly escaped from slavery and then went on to help free many more. Her inspiration was her faith – she believed that she had great potential, and she was not afraid to use this potential for good, for greatness, whatever intense difficulties she had to face. Today, let's believe that we have great potential, that there are so many possibilities of action we can take to improve our lives, and the lives of those around us.

May 17th

"Stay true to yourself, yet always be open to learn. Work hard, and never give up on your dreams, even when nobody else believes they can come true but you. These are not clichés but real tools you need no matter what you do in life to stay focused on your path"

Phillip Sweet

I know it can be so tough sometimes getting ourselves started on something or keeping going, but by encouraging ourselves to push forward our hard work moves us ever towards our chosen goals, and in turn it pays dividends in the self-belief that we come to feel in our hearts. A self-belief that we can come back to when we most need it.

May 18th

"Clouds come floating into my life, no longer to carry rain or usher storm, but to add colour to my sunset sky"

Rabindranath Tagore

Once we overcome our obstacles we can view them as vehicles for our growth. What if we started viewing obstacles as the foundation for our growth in the midst of facing them? To believe in turning the poisons in our life into the medicine of our growth, is the way to have faith in oneself. Let's refuse to give up, refuse to be defeated, whatever we face. Let's lead this noble path of tenacity, of the courage to keep on. This potential is inherent in you, in me. This potential is what makes us all great, and it often takes suffering to realise how truly great we can be. Let's never be defeated and always use our struggles to show what the words 'victory in life' truly mean.

May 19th

"One of the most sincere forms of respect is actually listening to what another has to say"

Bryant H. McGill

Good listening is, paradoxically, complicated and easy at the same time. It's hard to do, but essentially it rests on a simple principle. It is empathy, it is really caring about what someone is saying and really caring about them, as they say it. This is true respect. In our interactions today, let's bring sincerity into our ability to understand first, really taking in the heart of where the other person is coming from, before we comment to support or challenge the views of others, in order to show a deep respect for who they are and their position of interest.

May 20th

"What is easily done can be easily undone. To move steadily forward on one's chosen path, step after step, whether or not others are watching; to meet difficulties with the steady, relentless strength of ceaselessly flowing water— such firmness of purpose, such integrity and perseverance builds a foundation that can never be compromised"

Daisaku Ikeda

We cannot help but be shaken by some obstacles. At such times, let us hold strong to the sails of our inner self. Let's hold on, for long enough, until courage, strength and our capacity to believe in ourselves returns. It is then that we can use our strength to adjust the sails to life's winds, so that we continue on our path to personal growth for our own happiness and the happiness of those around us.

May 21st

"Dead people receive more flowers than the living because regret is stronger than gratitude"

Anne Frank

Gratitude is the most beautiful thing in the world. It expresses an acknowledgement that, fundamentally, all is connected. Furthermore, we find our place in the world, because of what we have and because of those who have acted on our behalf. Anne Frank is right though, regret strikes like an arrow in the heart, debilitating in its sting, whilst our gratitude is only getting into first gear. Let's take a moment today, perhaps right now, to consider something done for us: somebody, or something in our life that we really couldn't do without. Let's imagine everything good that comes from having that one thing in our life. An antidote to the unnecessary pain of regret, may this feeling of gratitude rise up in us, like a warmth in our being.

May 22nd

"If the minds of living beings are impure, their land is also impure, but if their minds are pure, so is their land. There are not two lands, pure or impure in themselves. The difference lies solely in the good or evil of our minds"

Nichiren Daishonin

Peace scholar, Elise Boulding, argues that 5 percent of active and committed members of a society can ultimately transform that society in its entirety. We only have to look at history to see that small groups of people – in comparison with the general population – such as civil rights activists, suffragettes, abolitionists, activists for independence, have rocked societies. They were once a small number of committed individuals. For this reason, let us never underestimate our role as bastions of peace, transforming the hearts of others around us, where we are, with our words, in spite of the geopolitical circumstances we may find ourselves in.

May 23rd

"Goodness is about character - integrity, honesty, kindness, generosity, moral courage, and the like. More than anything else, it is about how we treat other people"

Dennis Prager

Sometimes we disparage ourselves by saying we can't do x or y. But ultimately we, like all others, can make a difference, can make someone else smile, can be an ear to listen, can give charitably (perhaps through our precious time) to others. We can be kind and this is where our self-esteem should have the opportunity to be just as strong as anybody else's. We can all be kind to others in our daily interactions and reap the benefits of feeling positive about ourselves too. Let's allow ourselves to feel good as we sincerely interact with others around us today.

May 24th

"A friend is what the heart needs all the time"

Henry Van Dyke

Let's reaffirm the beautiful friendships we have, and build new ones too, when sincere interactions arise. Friendship found with friends of old, friends of new, families, and relationships, and in connections we are yet to form. Building that level of trust and sincerity where we can be ourselves and where the other person can be too, is true caring, consideration and understanding of another. Let's continue to consolidate and create connections like this day in, day out, wherever we are.

May 25th

"Our greatest glory is not in never failing, but in rising up every time we fail"

Ralph Waldo Emerson

Worded like this, we cannot fail to realise intellectually that victory is to continue, is to pick oneself up, is to rise again. We have difficulty believing this, we have difficulty following this mantra, and tend to blame, ridicule and doubt instead, each time we fall. Today let's remember these words, let's live by them, let's catch that negativity berating us when we fall, and take a minute to breathe, calm, and reconstruct our inner dialogue: we are human, and what makes us shine as humans, is what we choose to do next.

May 26th

"However difficult life may seem, there is always something you can do and succeed at"

Stephen Hawking

This quote is the antithesis of the classic 'things could be worse'. When someone says to us, 'things could be worse' perhaps giving us an obvious example, it may at best contextualise our suffering, but at worse it can add to it further, by making us feel silly for having natural and legitimate feelings. What Hawking says above is a completely different way to deal with suffering – the beautiful sentiment of his words is a call to action: a call to create value where we can! If we can use our suffering as an impetus to actually do something either about it, or about something else that we can change, then we can get a sense of empowerment that begins to shake off the hopelessness we originally felt in the first place.

May 27th

"Did I offer peace today? Did I bring a smile to someone's face? Did I say words of healing? Did I let go of my anger and resentment? Did I forgive? Did I love? These are the real questions. I must trust that the little bit of love that I sow now will bear many fruits"

Henri Nouwen

This quote shows that life is about the actions we take for ourselves and others, and that we do not have to see the fruits that oneself or others will receive from such actions to justify their significance. That is what faith means: trusting that if we keep trying to make a difference to our own situation and that of others, eventually we will suceed. As long as we try to bring happiness to ourselves, our families and others, we are going to grow more resilient to life's buffeting winds each day.

May 28th

"You must do the things you think you cannot do"

Eleanor Roosevelt

Working to achieve our own human revolution, our own inner transformation – the changes we bring about in ourselves that we didn't think were possible – can take arduous struggle and determination. As we challenge what life has to offer us, we grow in courage and in the belief that we can rise to meet all of our obstacles. When we start to gain this kind of belief, we work towards absolute happiness. When we understand the impermanence of all things, we see that change is always possible and that we must begin to grow to become the person we wish to be.

May 29th

"I learned that courage was not the absence of fear, but the triumph over it. The brave man is not he who does not feel afraid, but he who conquers that fear"

Nelson Mandela

Courage really does not exist when we're unafraid or untroubled. If you're carrying on despite the difficulties you're facing right now then you are by definition courageous. Please continue to persevere in the face and of adversity. You will look back with pride for pushing through your difficulties.

May 30th

"I've been absolutely terrified every moment of my life - and I've never let it keep me from doing a single thing I wanted to do"

Georgia O'Keeffe

We need the kind of courage that O'Keeffe describes to be truly fulfilled. It does not matter if an external obstacle gets in the way of our dreams and aspirations; the very nature of such a hurdle emerging is proof of how far we have come; it is how we react to it that matters. Mandela echoes O'Keeffe with his eternal statement that "courage is not the absence of fear it is the overcoming of it". Let's have the courage to pursue our chosen paths today, being who we truly are, and winning in our hearts against whatever twists and turns we face.

May 31st

"Positive feelings come from being honest about yourself and accepting your personality, and physical characteristics, warts and all; and, from belonging to a family that accepts you without question"

Willard Scott

As you read this, please know that whoever you are, wherever you are, and as you are, I am wishing to connect with your sincere, unfiltered and honest, personality, character, and life. Beyond the sum of our actions, choices, and appearance, are our true selves. The true us, the real us, which combines the negative and positive aspects of ourselves. Please let go of your negative feelings about yourself and be proud to be you. Please accept yourself exactly as you are so that you can begin to love the special person within. For I am sending the warmest of wishes to you right now.

June 1st

"Until such time as the world ends, we will act as though it intends to spin on"

Nick Fury

We have overcome difficult things before, and we will again. We are stronger than we ever know. Sometimes it feels as though we lose the gravity of our self-worth and begin to lose touch with reality. Deep within us, the latent strength is waiting to move us forward from our suffering and spin into happiness again. Let us stay strong and take refuge, and indeed self respect, in everything we have overcome to date, when times have been at their toughest. Let us keep going in the knowledge that the world keeps going and so will we.

June 2nd

"Never believe that a few caring people can't change the world. For, indeed, that's all who ever have"

Margaret Mead

Elise Boulding estimated that most big movements that change society come from the ground up and generally require only 5% of the population. I cannot begin to imagine the untold suffering and strength that was required to get movements such as women's suffrage, black civil rights, and Indian independence to gain their momentum. Beautiful hearted people behind the scenes, attending meetings, taking action, but also, day to day, living out their aims, through their sincere interactions with others. In the spiritual interpersonal malaise of our times, let our interactions be a little light. With a little peace in our hearts, let's fight to overcome darkness, where we are, with our words and our smiles.

"Happiness does not come from doing easy work but from the afterglow of satisfaction that comes after the achievement of a difficult task that demanded our best."

Theodore Isaac Rubin

Our best is that which we can give, there and then. Our best is that which we possess as strength at any given moment. Sometimes our reserves run low. Instead of berating ourselves, we should know that if we are struggling, then our best will look very different, but we should still be so proud of our efforts, however small, as they are putting us slowly back on track. May we glow today from our efforts to take on that which the day throws at us and may we have a smile for whatever we achieve through our sincere personal endeavours today.

June 4th

"We know what we are, but know not what we may be"

William Shakespeare

Every act of kindness, and every experience we have, contributes to our ever-changing self. Think of who you are now compared to who you were ten, or even five, years ago. The truth of impermanence is that we are ever-changing in personality, in wishes, goals, beliefs, and this truth of change, gives rise to hope, excitement and opportunity. I hope we can continue to believe in our ever-changing self and find freedom in this innate truth.

June 5th

"Let us be anxious to do well, not for selfish praise but to honour and advance the cause, the work we have taken up"

Florence Nightingale

May our wish to succeed become a healthy catalyst for positive action. I hope though that we can live free of the internal stress or guilt that so often clouds the moments in which we quite naturally make mistakes or fall short of our aims. To try and to fail is still internally beautiful. Let us strive towards our goals and objectives with the kindness of a friend, knowing that unless we embrace ourselves each time we fall, we won't be able to flourish. Whether we get there or not, our relationship towards ourselves will always be the most important journey of all.

June 6th

"My wish for you is that you continue. Continue to be who and how you are, to astonish a mean world, with acts of kindness"

Maya Angelou

These words might seem like, sentiments, but they are so true. Wherever you are, please continue in the midst of difficulty, or in the midst of good times. Keep going, keep smiling – where possible – and when the moments arise, spread that kindness in words, and sincerity, like it multiplies back to you. For this is how we are remembered, and this is indeed how we astonish and spread joy, while we are here.

June 7th

"If you're trying to achieve, there will be roadblocks. I've had them; everybody has had them. But obstacles don't have to stop you. If you run into a wall, don't turn around and give up. Figure out how to climb it, go through it, or work around it"

Michael Jordan

If you have an obstacle in your life, think of the Newtonian rule that every action has an equal and opposite reaction; it probably means that you have made some effort in one of the many areas in your life and have thus come across the friction, the gravity, that comes from trying to move forward. Let today's roadblocks bring a wry smile in the knowledge that pushing against the wall in front of us is proof of the progress we have made thus far.

June 8th

"Bad things do happen; how I respond to them defines my character and the quality of my life. I can choose to sit in perpetual sadness, immobilized by the gravity of my loss, or I can choose to rise from the pain and treasure the most precious gift I have - life itself"

Walter Anderson

At times life is incredibly tough. If we first choose to move forward then we begin to develop the strength to grow as a person, as we journey into, and through, the difficulty head on, one day at a time. Let's grow in courage, in wisdom and most importantly in compassion, as we navigate our difficulties with hope ever in our hearts.

June 9th

"There is some good in the worst of us and some evil in the best of us. When we discover this, we are less prone to hate our enemies"

Martin Luther King, Jr.

This is an elemental belief for true dialogue in society. Understanding this truth, makes the world more peaceful each day and helps us to care more for those around us. We will have difficult interactions at times, and we will find people that do not respect us as they should. When we don't see eye to eye with colleagues, with friends, let's try to find it in our hearts to believe that there is more to this person and, over time, grow to see another side of them – a side not defined by their behaviour, not defined by the suffering they have caused. A side we can relate to, believe in – a side we can come to slowly respect. If not for them, let's do this for us. So we can either let go and move on, or even change things.

June 10th

"Hardship and ease walk hand in hand in this world, and embracing them both as being from the same benevolent source ensures that we walk with gratitude for our blessings and gratefulness for our challenges"

Hamza Yusuf

It may feel contrary to our experience, but there is no doubt that if we can feel gratitude for our ability to challenge our circumstances, then we grow in our ability to do just that, and if we find appreciation in that which we have, we can build on that too. Let's find it in us to open our hearts today to embrace that which we have, and that which we are yet to become.

June 11th

> "The main thing is to be proud of the work you do, to live true to yourself. Activity is another name for happiness. What's important is that you give free, unfettered play to your unique talents, that you live with the full radiance of your being. This is what it means to be truly alive"

Daisaku Ikeda

I hope we feel totally alive today and engaged in what we are doing, whether it be, within the home, at work, through study or through meeting others. Activity is to be in the moment, activity is to be engaged with a thing that means something to us, either by virtue of the joy we get from doing it, or by virtue of the longer-term joy that it creates. Today, let's get stuck into whatever life has to bring.

June 12th

"How wonderful it is that nobody need wait a single moment before starting to improve the world"

Anne Frank

Let's use as many of our moments in a way that supports our belief in potential, our belief in change. Let's make a difference to our lives and the lives of others. Every little thing you do matters more than you will ever know. So let's live out today with a deep respect for this principle, a deep respect for our lives and our potential.

June 13th

"True friendship multiplies the good in life and divides its evils. Strive to have friends, for life without friends is like life on a desert island... to find one real friend in a lifetime is good fortune; to keep him is a blessing"

Baltasar Gracián

Let's be that friend today who is sincere, caring and there. Let's be like that in our interactions with everyone we are engaged in conversation with: showing kindness and credibility. May this way of living multiply the goodness of our lives and divide our negativity too.

June 14th

"If you want others to be happy, practice compassion. If you want to be happy, practice compassion"

The Dalai Lama

Numerous studies show that as we show compassion to others, as we act altruistically with a view that we can become happy as we help others to become happy, we contribute positively to our own well-being. Why? Perhaps because in a sea of darkness we realise that we contain a whole load of light, and thus our self-esteem and self-belief are increasingly buoyed by the rising tide of smiles we see on the faces of others. Let's lift others today, whilst paying attention to our needs and interests too, so that one does not overshadow the other.

June 15th

"The moment one definitely commits oneself, then providence moves too. All sorts of things occur to help one that would never otherwise have occurred. A whole stream of events issues from the decision, raising in one's favour all manner of unforeseen incidents and meetings and material assistance, which no man could have dreamt would have come his way. I have learned a deep respect for one of Goethe's couplets: Whatever you can do, or dream you can, begin it. Boldness has genius, power, and magic in it!"

W.H. Murray

Let's remain ever committed to the struggles we face, with confidence and courage, for ourselves and those around us. Let's make proud all those whom our actions affect, by committing to them with an intense determination and tenacity today.

June 16th

"We can easily forgive a child who is afraid of the dark; the real tragedy of life is when men are afraid of the light"

Plato

Within us all is an inner light which is illuminated by self-compassion, self-love and patience. These three qualities can be so difficult to unlock if we have grown up believing that we are unworthy of love or that we are not truly deserving of our own respect unless we ourselves change. Today though, I hope that each of us can step towards the light of inner acceptance embracing the view that in order to make any changes in our life we must first accept our inner brilliance that has been there since the day we were born, a greatness which cannot be destroyed.

June 17th

"The greatest glory in living lies not in never falling, but in rising every time we fall"

Nelson Mandela

With this quote I wish you a day of strength, resilience and self-belief. The self-determination to keep going, with knowledge that this in itself is victory. Our victory is a victory over doubt, a victory of the heart.

June 18th

"Knowing is not enough; we must apply. Willing is not enough; we must do"

Johann Wolfgang von Goethe

Action is another word for happiness as Daisaku Ikeda says. It is in doing, in being, that we truly live out our lives. If words and thought are the shadow, and what we do for ourselves and others day to day, is the person. Let's choose to live today, with confidence in the seeds that our actions sow. A confidence that we need not be restricted by any preconceptions of who we are, for through action we can grow to be who we wish to be.

June 19th

"If you know the enemy and know yourself you need not fear the results of a hundred battles"

Sun Tzu

In knowing your enemy you are one step closer to victory. The battle I'm engaged in, along with a significant minority of the world's inhabitants, is the battle for pure equality and subsequently peace, through one to one dialogue, education and culture. When we deny the dignity of each human life, of our life, we give in to doubt. Let's know our internal enemy of doubt, fear and disrespect. Let's rise above our doubt, to the universal respect-worthy human that we are, deserving of our own love, our appreciation and respect, not because of what we have done, or who we are, but because of what we possess, and who we can become. Let's respect our inner self today.

June 20th

"Life isn't about finding yourself. Life is about creating yourself"

George Bernard Shaw

This quote reminds us that it is we who are the protagonists in our own unique journeys. This creation of self, this act of initiative, this change and growth, comes through believing that we are ever-changing and always becoming our future selves, with every day a new chance, for new decisions and new growth. Let's show more of who we are and what we truly represent, in our interactions today.

June 21st

"Perfection is not attainable, but if we chase perfection we can catch excellence"

Vince Lombardi

Whilst we don't want to get bogged down by perfection in activities which are time-restricted, we can take our lives, one action at a time, one event at a time, one day at a time. Let's strive for the excellence of being engaged in what we are doing, holding off that which will come later until later, so that we organically become more in tune with our day. With kindness to ourselves for the many times we don't achieve this, let's nonetheless pursue an authenticity of being there in the midst of our days, fully engaged in what we can achieve.

June 22nd

"When there is harmony between the mind, heart and resolution then nothing is impossible"

The Rig Veda

It may be that we are plunged into darkness within our circumstances today, or it may be that we are in full flow and confidence. Wherever we are in the midst of all life has to throw at us, let us never forget this sentiment and keep going, knowing that this is even more of an accomplishment than the end goal itself.

June 23rd

"Don't find fault, find a remedy"

Henry Ford

My greatest wish is that you can keep finding a way through. My deepest prayer is that you can be courageous in spirit and always impart hope by doing so. Hope for yourself, and hope for others. For hope leads to action, and action leads to value. Let's create value where we are, as we are, beginning to remedy all that tries to pull us down as we create a dawn that sheds light on the darkness.

June 24th

"It does not matter how slowly you go, as long as you do not stop"

Confucius

Let's aim for progress, not the finished article. Let's challenge the difficult circumstances that arise, fighting to overcome that which is in front of us, step by step, action by action, not yet knowing where the road will take us. If we have already taken the first step, we are already on the road. One foot in front of the other, let's push through the darkness with a lantern of self-belief, ever lighting the way, so that each day we can move one step forward.

June 25th

"You've done it before and you can do it now. See the positive possibilities. Redirect the substantial energy of your frustration and turn it into positive, effective, unstoppable determination"

Ralph Marston

When we are locked in adversity, we can look back to the numerous examples of that which we have overcome. When it is others we love and care for that are engaged in struggle, when the time is right and they have been fully understood and heard, we can also share with them how far they have come. Let our precious victories of the heart up to this date inspire not only us, but others too.

June 26th

"A warm smile is the universal language of kindness"

William Arthur Ward

Let's keep smiling when we meet and greet others. Let's also show sincerity when we're having a tough time and are asked how it is going. Smiling when possible really allows others to know we see them and we recognise their humanity. It affirms that they matter; it reminds us that we matter too.

June 27th

"Keep your face to the sunshine and you cannot see a shadow"

Helen Keller

This incredible human being battled being deaf-blind to achieve so much in addition to her published political activism. This wouldn't have happened if she hadn't looked forward – to what she could do, to the next step, to value she could create, to the person she could become, having faith that each step she took would get her closer to there. Let's consider what we can do, and have faith in who we can slowly become.

June 28th

"No one can read with profit that which he cannot learn to read with pleasure"

Thomas Hardy

I really agree that you need to find pleasure in what you are doing – it pay huge dividends and increases your ability to do it. Sometimes to enjoy what we do requires a change in circumstances that we may have to commit to with our own effort, choice and will. Other times it takes a fresh look, a new perspective on that which we have. During my studies, years ago, I loved reading anything to do with philosophy. It was not a chore and whilst other subjects eventually fell by the wayside, I did excel in Philosophy because of this love. I know that we can never find each and every thing we do fascinating or exciting, but let's find and inject interest and enjoyment into important areas of our lives when we can, so that we can derive more pleasure day by day.

June 29th

"The world is a drama, staged in a dream"

Guru Nanak

It is my fervent wish that we can positively face our challenges, understanding the bigger picture, so that we can find joy and a wry smile in the midst of our adversity. I hope that today you are able to dig deep, stand back and take in all that that this day has to offer.

June 30th

"Always remember that you are absolutely unique. Just like everyone else"

Jim Wright

I love this quote, not just because it's light-hearted, but also because it speaks the absolute truth: a truth that everyone should act on. We are all special from the word go. Our lives are deeply dignified and if we act towards each other with this belief, we create a far better world than the one we find. Let's act towards others with this knowledge today.

July 1st

"Failure is success if we learn from it"

Malcolm Forbes

This is the key to developing who we are. Opening the door to our personal growth. Let's keep in our hearts the knowledge that each failure is a stepping stone to success if we view it as a lesson and begin to move things forward.

July 2nd

"You, yourself, as much as anybody in the entire universe, deserve your love and affection"

Shakyamuni Buddha

How true this is. Yet we so often fail to show this level of kindness when we don't quite get things right. Very often we are quick to curse our actions, to berate ourselves for a mistake or failure. Next time we catch ourselves doing this, let's stop ourselves and think about what we are doing. Let's leave behind our misgivings and treat ourselves with the kindness of a friend, and say. 'You stumbled, old friend, but you can shine once again. Keep believing in yourself.' Let's grant ourselves the kindness we deserve today.

July 3rd

"The greatest heroes are those who do their duty in the daily grind of domestic affairs whilst the world whirls as a maddening dreidel"

Florence Nightingale

The true heroes of life are those who live through life's most arduous struggles, not looking for praise, not looking for glory. The mother who works two jobs to make sure her children are fed, the person who keeps on going despite the fact their mental health is at rock bottom. Picking yourself back up, continuing to keep going despite everything appearing to be against you is to shine as a human being, and no other person in the world can ever shake that truth.

July 4th

"We must be realists in our brains while keeping the flame of idealism burning in our hearts"

Johan Galtung

When we cast our eyes over reality, according to whichever medium and media it is presented to us, we see darkness and negativity leading the way. Unfortunately there is darkness in the world, and we must be realistic about this. Nonetheless, we know that good acts outweigh evil acts, day in, day out, but good news, is not the news – it doesn't sell, it doesn't bring headlines. The truth is, there is more good than evil. The truth is, most people, just like us, want things to change. All we have to do is concentrate on our small corner of the world, do our thing, bring a little light, and let that light catch on, like wildfire. This is where our optimism should lie.

July 5th

"Sometimes a loss is the best thing that can happen. It teaches you what you should have done next time"

Snoop Dogg

Just in case you have a tough day today, think, what can I learn from this? How can I use this to grow as person? Perhaps it will help you to help others too.

July 6th

"Wisdom is the right use of knowledge. To know is not to be wise. Many men know a great deal, and are all the greater fools for it. There is no fool so great a fool as a knowing fool. But to know how to use knowledge is to have wisdom."

Charles Spurgeon

There can be no true wisdom without compassion for others. Wisdom is seeing that the others around us matter as equally and particularly as we do. If today, and in the days to come, we can find it in our hearts to reach out and offer positive words, or actions, in the situations we find ourselves, then that which we do know will come to bear the fruit of wisdom, which others around us will increasingly see.

July 7th

"Things turn out best for the people who make the best of the way things turn out"

John Wooden

Although Wooden uses an element of humour, he speaks an honourable truth. That is, we are dealt what we are dealt each day, and if we rise to meet it we are far more likely to swing the odds in our favour: to create value, where we stand, as we are, and build happiness from the ground up.

July 8th

"The measure of who we are is what we do with what we have"

Vince Lombardi

One of the most important things in the world, which we have little of in the end, is time. As life passes in the blink of an eye, as a cosmic moment in relation to the eternity of the universe itself, we must make arduous efforts to use the time we have, to do that which really matters to us. If we are engaged with family, may there be inner harmony. If we are engaged in struggle, let's fight with our soul. If we are working, let's bring light there. Whatever we are doing today, let's not forget that time is beautifully limited, and enjoy that which we have today.

July 9th

"One of the most beautiful qualities of true friendship is to understand and to be understood"

Lucius Annaeus Seneca

Please always be there for your friends, family and colleagues, even if you fall out or have disagreements. If you always have each other's best interests at heart, and you can grow in the belief that friendship based on trust truly lightens life's difficulties and heightens life's joys.

July 10th

"The purpose of our lives is to be happy"

Dalai Lama

Let's not lose sight of this whatever gets in the way. Let's work hard to overcome the obstacles to our happiness, as in overcoming them – growing in belief, strength and courage – is happiness itself.

July 11th

"The greatest trap in our life is not success, popularity or power, but self-rejection"

Henri Nouwen

Underneath everything we have ever said and done is who we really are, and this pure compassionate self is available to everyone to bring forth. Let's take a moment to fully believe in our pure self, beyond doubts, delusion and comparisons. Let's use this understanding of how special we are deep down to look forward and believe in our potential to take on our situation as we are.

July 12th

"One way to get the most out of life is to look upon it as an adventure"

William Feather

If our lives have every potential to be an adventure then we are the protagonists. Let's ride the ups and the downs, let's suffer what we have to suffer, but grow in the process. Let's enjoy what there is to enjoy, and savour who we become. May we ever believe in ourselves as the protagonists as we boldly and positively face our circumstances today.

July 13th

"All the beautiful sentiments in the world weigh less than a single lovely action"

James Russell Lowell

What a lovely quote telling us to do something lovely for someone every day. It could be picking up the phone to someone we've meant to call, it could be sending a message or writing a letter in that very special analogue way. The truth is it can be smaller than that, it really can be a natural organic action, or words, that feel right in the situation we find ourselves in at some point today. And if we feel that we cannot because our suffering is too deep, it may be that such an action creates the first bit of light in the tunnel we find ourselves in. Whatever our situation, let's create positive actions in our lives.

July 14th

"Now and then it's good to pause in our pursuit of happiness and just be happy"

Guillaume Apollinaire

I think Apollinaire is alluding to true gratitude in the moment. I hope we can make time for a moment to pause today and just feel truly happy, even if just for a while. It makes you realise that the deep feeling of absolute happiness, as opposed to short-term relative happiness, comes from within not from without. Circumstances are so important, and changing them at times, can be so vital. Nonetheless, happiness is a state of mind, so let's take one minute today, to breathe, to feel, to acknowledge that which we have deep in the depths of our lives.

July 15th

"Where there's hope, there's life. It fills us with fresh courage and makes us strong again"

Anne Frank

When we are facing difficulty we can start to wish for a surge of courage to face the situation. If that surge doesn't come remember that to face the situation requires in itself a deep and underlying courage. By having the courage to face our difficulties one day at a time, we will create such an opportunity for a surge of hope to emerge.

July 16th

"Between stimulus and response there is a space. In that space is our power to choose our response. In our response lies our growth and our freedom"

Viktor E. Frankl

Today's encouragement is from psychologist and holocaust survivor Viktor Frankl. His story is incredible and his quotes are inspirational. He has written an incredible account of his time in the concentration camps, where on occasion he managed to raise the spirits of others. He is saying that the very difficulties and obstacles we want to wish away can become part of our growth and our eventual freedom, if we can view the facing and overcoming of them as having profound meaning in our lives.

July 17th

"Give light, and the darkness will disappear of itself"

Desiderius Erasmus

One important aspect of our happiness is to bring a little light to the days of others, even in the smallest ways. Let's create a little light, a little joy, whenever we see the opportunity. I hope that we are able to do so today and reap what we sow in the happiness it will bring in our hearts.

July 18th

"There is no passion to be found playing small – in settling for a life that is less than the one you are capable of living"

Nelson Mandela

What do you want to do in your life that you have yet to begun? Maybe it's fear that is stopping you pursuing your dreams. Maybe it is life's responsibilities that stop you from beginning. If you can, each week find a little time, however small, for your dream, so that you can lay the groundwork of knowing what you want to get out of life. So, when the time is right to accelerate your plans, you can go go go. Let's start playing big with our dreams as soon as is right and beginning the small steps to make them happen, whether these be writing a little each week, saving a bit of money month by month, making the contacts for future business plans, beginning to cut down on something we want to give up. Let's begin the groundwork for our later successes, with the notion that our efforts will bring us great benefits regardless of the long-term outcome.

July 19th

"The Earth and Sun do not hurry; they follow their own path at their own pace. If the Earth were to accelerate and complete one rotation in three hours instead of twenty-four, we would be in big trouble! The most important thing in life, too, is to find a sure and certain path and confidently advance along it"

Daisaku Ikeda

This quote reminds us to advance along our own path at a pace right for who we are, where we are, and the circumstances we find ourselves in. There may be many stages on our journey of growth, and we may transition from one role to another, from time to time, but the key is to keep going, to adapt and make changes where and when we need to. Pace means little if we are not true to ourselves. Let's be ourselves today. May our lives take the direction that best fits our needs, values, and interests that we hold true to our hearts.

July 20th

"Far away there in the sunshine are my highest aspirations. I may not reach them, but I can look up and see their beauty, believe in them, and try to follow where they lead"

Louisa May Alcott

Let's go after our dreams and aspirations with the courage to overcome our fears, for when we fall we get back up each time anew, continuing on our journey. So let's pursue today, with a small step forward, that which we wish to see bloom in our lives, through our decisions, our words and actions, allowing to slowly come to the fore, the person we truly wish to be.

July 21st

"The self is not something ready-made, but something in continuous formation through choice of action"

John Dewey

John Dewey, the American educational philosopher, argued for the uniqueness of each individual and their capacity for growth. As his quote here alludes, this growth, this self-reformation, is life-long. So let's not give up on ourselves today, let's reignite our beliefs that until our last, we are constantly, growing, changing, expanding and developing who we are.

July 22nd

"Without a struggle, there can be no progress"

Frederick Douglass

Whilst we wish for a life without struggle, the four sufferings of Buddhism – of birth, aging, sickness and death – are incumbent on us all. In fact, the first of the four sufferings refers to how in order to live, we must be born, and therefore struggle, even before coming to the other three sufferings. As there must be struggle of some kind for us, let there be joy in overcoming it. If there must be struggle, let there be growth and strength in facing it. May we find a special place in our hearts to be proud of ourselves, to be happy in ourselves, when we do find the strength to keep going in the midst of difficulty.

July 23rd

"If people knew how hard I worked to achieve my mastery, it wouldn't seem so wonderful at all"

Michelangelo

It is really profound to hear this from someone we assume to be a natural genius. There is no doubt in his talent, but he is categorically telling us that his masterpieces were one big struggle to keep going, and going, and going. One moment at a time. Whilst we may not be attempting to create a masterpiece per se, we are trying to create something equally as meaningful: a life of happiness and strength. So let's not believe that some have special abilities to be happy, let's instead believe that when we look back at the happiness we've created, the struggle we never gave up on, it was our hard work, our determination to not give in, that made all the difference.

July 24th

"Perseverance is not a long race; it is many short races one after the other"

Walter Elliot

I think this has real resonance with everyone, for if we face and overcome one small challenge or struggle at a time it is amazing what we have achieved when we look back. So let's push on with whatever today will bring, proud of the many short races we have run to date.

July 25th

"The beginning of purpose is found in creating something that only you understand"

Tyler Joseph

Our long-term joy and happiness comes from losing ourselves in that goal, that ambition, that drive towards something we care about deeply. It is to be lost in that which we love, as lost as a child dancing with joy on a summers day. Let's move ever towards those goals, ambitions, and people in our lives too, whom we love. Let's lose ourselves in that which we love.

July 26th

"I am determined to be cheerful and happy in whatever situation I may find myself. For I have learned that the greater part of our misery or unhappiness is determined not by our circumstance but by our disposition"

Martha Washington

Even though it can be extremely difficult to face tough circumstances with a positive forward-looking attitude, if we can muster the inner strength to do so, we really can transform many a situation and forge our character. I hope today, that we can find this strength in our hearts to find happiness in adversity.

July 27th

"A journey of a thousand miles begins with one step."

Lao Tzu

The more and more you face and overcome difficulties, the more and more strength you develop to continue doing so. It builds and builds, so let's start with the small difficulties today and win where we stand, for these are the steps on our incredible journey of a thousand miles to come.

July 28th

"Age wrinkles the body, quitting wrinkles the soul"

Douglas MacArthur

With quotes such as these, we can look to the truth inherent in the sentiment that is expressed, rather than the literal expression. I say this because sometimes it is of course wisdom, to quit someone, to move on. What MacAthur is instead referring to is when we are engaged in a struggle, a struggle we must win, we must not give up. Sometimes in life an obstacle or suffering cannot be changed per se, but that is why continuing on, keeping going, expresses our greatest vitality, our inner youth, for it allows us to grow in strength and eventually change our attitudes themselves, in order to become the protagonist in our struggle.

July 29th

"He who is not every day conquering some fear has not learned the secret of life"

Ralph Waldo Emerson

To live our lives fully, is to accept who we are by conquering our doubts and overcoming our fears. We all have inherent dignity and are worthy of respect deep down. What is it that gives each human such incredible potential? It is our capacity to use what we have been through, the fears we have overcome in our lives, to empathise with others, to be kind, to stand up courageously and to show others that whatever we go through we never give up. By doing that we will not fail to find happiness for ourselves and will inspire others to do the same too.

July 30th

"When a tree has been transplanted, though fierce winds may blow, it will not topple if it has a firm stake to hold it up. But even a tree that has grown up in place may fall over if its roots are weak. Even a feeble person will not stumble if those supporting him are strong, but a person of considerable strength when alone, may fall down on an uneven path"

Nichiren Daishonin

This reminds us how very important friendship is. We must be relied upon to support those around us, and those around us to support us too. Life, which is full of joy, can yet be difficult, emotionally draining, stressful or promote within us any number of other feelings. Let's never retreat though. Let's always be there for each other. Let's listen to others we care for and always be supportive, let us be the stake in the ground so that other people can grow strong, and so they can support us when we need them too.

July 31st

"Nobody made a greater mistake than he who did nothing because he could do only a little"

Edmund Burke

So many of us think of what we cannot achieve, what we cannot do, and begin to undervalue and play down our undertakings. In doing this we begin to lose passion for that which is important to us and the many others we come into contact with in our daily lives. It is the difference we do make that defines us. We can do so much if we just concentrate on what we can do. Let's do just that today, giving full play to our ability to make small but significant differences that lift others too, day by day.

August 1st

"Noble deeds that are concealed are most esteemed"

Blaise Pascal

Pascal has a great point. If we are kind to others and despite external benefit then by deduction any such benefit must be internal. This means that the positivity we feel from helping others, and how we grow and develop as a person, well up within us. We are able to do actions that bring joy, though we might believe these go unnoticed. If we are helping others out of a pure and sincere wish for their happiness, we ourselves genuinely grow and strengthen our foundations for our own happiness too.

August 2nd

"You will never be happy if you continue to search for what happiness consists of. You will never live if you are looking for the meaning of life"

Albert Camus

I think Camus makes an excellent point: that happiness is action, happiness is the purpose of actions, so let's get on with the hard work of being happy and continue to fight to overcome any difficulty we are facing. Let's create causes that are excellent in themselves rather than worrying too much over where they lead.

August 3rd

"Some people only ask others to do something. I believe that, why should I wait for someone else? Why don't I take a step and move forward"

Malala Yousafzai

Sometimes a good idea arises in one's conscious, e.g. to do something of note for oneself or someone else: a really positive idea about something you want to do, whether to better yourself or to lift the heart of another. Incredibly, despite your noble plan, "wouldn't it be great if I..." you will quickly find that you are doubting yourself. "What if they think x? I haven't really got time to do that because of y. Maybe it won't have any positive effect." By appreciating that our self-doubt is an internal protective force that can sometimes stop us taking action, let's be open to the possibility that we can and do make a difference. Concentrating on the cause we make, rather than the effect we are yet to know, frees us to act with a pure sincerity.

August 4th

"Life is 10% what happens to you and 90% how you react to it"

Charles R. Swindoll

This is an extremely important quote that allows us to understand that we do create our happiness from that which is presented to us. Let's create value and find happiness in what is in front of us. If the darkness is strong in our situation, let's vow to be the light, to lift ourselves and others, no matter how long that inner transformation takes. If the sun shines at the moment, let's use that as an ideal opportunity to spread that light further and strengthen our connections with those around us.

August 5th

"It is not because things are difficult that we do not dare, it is because we do not dare that things are difficult"

Seneca

Whilst this is no easy to surmount feat, there is a truth in our ability to change our perception of difficulty when we view it as an opportunity to be overcome; when we give our difficulty profound meaning. If we face our lives and any struggles within them with great strength and courage, the obstacles themselves become a more enriching part of our growth, to the point where we can even begin to find exhilaration as mountaineers of life, arduously scaling it's summits.

August 6th

"Nobody in life gets exactly what they thought they were going to get. But if you work really hard and you're kind, amazing things will happen"

Conan O'Brien

We have to show kindness to others, but in a way that we do not forget our own needs in the progress. If we look after ourselves, with enough rest, support and all the vitals of life, then there is more of us present, more of our wisdom and compassion to give. Whilst there are so many obstacles to being kind to others, namely reactions to us doing so, it is a true and worthy cause, and one to which numerous studies give testament to the benefits. So let's keep up the kindness to ourselves and others today.

August 7th

"Do your little bit of good where you are; it's those little bits of good put together that overwhelm the world"

Desmond Tutu

In doing a little bit of good for others, showing kindness and helping others, we gain real measurable psychological benefits according to numerous social scientific studies to date. Therefore, when these opportunities present themselves, let's help others and develop our characters in the process. Let's do "our little bit of good" by believing that we do have the capacity to give to others: it is part of what makes us great.

August 8th

"Ultimately, we are responsible for our own destiny. It may seem to us that our fate is predetermined, whether by our genes or by our environment. What really matters, however, is how we can improve ourselves from this moment forward, how we can change the circumstances that we find ourselves in. This enormous transformative force is what... [life] is all about. In this struggle lies the source of never-ending youth and vitality"

Daisaku Ikeda

In March, I mentioned that a phrase from Japan called 'honin myo', which essentially translates as 'from this moment on'. Buddhist scholar Daisaku Ikeda is referring to raising our attitude and esteem through our concerted effort over time to move forward, one step at a time. As we know, one step at a time, can be extremely difficult, sometimes even painful but when we look back on how far we have come we see the truth, that to continue is to succeed.

August 9th

"If I have seen further than others, it is by standing upon the shoulders of giants"

Isaac Newton

It is my struggles in life, both internal and external, that give me any legitimacy to write responses to quotes from such eminent thinkers. I write these responses from a deep and sincere wish for your happiness alongside mine. Let's continue to experience joy in this life, and if my responses to these quotes have in any way lifted you at any point, I will have to attribute that to the wisdom I have received through the writings of my incredible mentor Daisaku Ikeda, and also to that which I have gleaned from the 'giants' within the quotes of this book. Let's continue to stand on their shoulders together, one day at time, as we experience our personal growth.

August 10th

"Keep your face always toward the sunshine – and shadows will fall behind you"

Walt Whitman

The sentiment of this quote is profound – let's not just read it and forget it. Let's bring it to mind when we see the sun first thing in the morning. Let's pick a moment in our day, and see if our focus on the positive really does make that moment, or other such moments, more enjoyable, productive and give us the space for forward thinking.

August 11th

"Prayer does not change God, but it changes him who prays"

Søren Kierkegaard

I think this is a message about determination, vow and intention. Imagine I prayed for world peace sincerely with all my being every-day, or for the happiness of all others. I guess we know that these two things will not happen purely as a result purely of the prayers, but how about what might start happening on a personal level? Through such prayer one naturally aligns one's life with and towards these two things, thus changing how we think and feel too. Funnily enough, that's the Buddhist way of working towards peace. Feel free to pray for what you want in your heart, theist or not, for that will become more and more your focus in your waking hours.

August 12th

"Every human has four endowments - self awareness, conscience, independent will and creative imagination. These give us the ultimate human freedom... The power to choose, to respond, to change"

Stephen Covey

Living a life in which we use our imagination and will to respond positively to our environment, our circumstances, is a truly positive way to live. Let's enact positive change in our lives, moving towards the truth, where we feel able to take positive steps and bring forth an inner joy from courage, whatever we face. Let's take the first steps today towards this life-state by deciding the next positive action to take, as we are, wherever we are.

August 13th

"We can never obtain peace in the outer world until we make peace with ourselves"

The Dalai Lama

If we really want to make an impact on our surroundings, we must first have the biggest impact on ourselves. Let's truly believe in ourselves, not only our inherent dignity as human beings and our ability to help others, but also in the knowledge that we've had struggles before, and can see how far we have come. Let's believe that the wall in front of us, is actually proof of our inner greatness; the task that lies ahead is going to reveal that greatness as we strive to succeed and move forward.

August 14th

"Optimism is the faith that leads to achievement. Nothing can be done without hope and confidence"

Helen Keller

Many a quote I use comes from this incredible figurehead, who overcome so much to shine. She argues that the most important things in life cannot be seen, but must be felt instead with the heart. I want us to have full confidence in our hearts; we cannot even begin to fathom how incredibly strong and courageous we are when we believe in our potential, truly and sincerely.

August 15th

"We must build dikes of courage to hold back the flood of fear"

Martin Luther King, Jr.

Let the dikes of courage be built from the victories and successes we have had when look back at the struggles live has given us so far. Let a dam of determination be built from our belief in our hearts of who we can become. As the flood of fear rises in our given difficulty or inner fight, let us not give in to doubt, but stand strong, seeking the opportunity to take bold action so that we can use the difficulty as an opportunity to grow, to shine.

August 16th

"Fill your paper with the breathings of your heart"

William Wordsworth

Let our lives be the paper and our compassion for who we and others are deep down be the pen. Live true to the person who you are in the depths of your being. This is no easy road, but if we strive to spread happiness, naturally, day by day, we ourselves create treasures which cannot be burned by fire or washed away by water: treasures of the heart.

August 17th

"I think one's feelings waste themselves in words; they ought all to be distilled into actions which bring results"

Florence Nightingale

No one is denying that words can ignite the potential for change by moving our hearts, and the hearts of others, but action is change itself manifest. So let's take such action today, as we are, wherever we are, in our own unique way, and if we are really struggling today, let us deem no action too small to take to move things in the right direction.

August 18th

"Action may not always bring happiness; but there is no happiness without action"

Benjamin Disraeli

Disraeli's thought is succinctly presented to us, yet it took time, effort, and reasoning to get to this point of truth. No action will guarantee our happiness, will guarantee we break free from any chains of difficulty or suffering. Nonetheless by taking action in the face of difficulty we are expressing what is to be human, for we are expressing our right to choose how we face suffering, and our right to work our way through it to create value and, where possible, joy.

August 19th

"But there was no need to be ashamed of tears, for tears bore witness that a man had the greatest of courage, the courage to suffer"

Viktor Frankl

Whilst suffering is painful by nature, let's not add to this burden by judging ourselves too. We are incredibly special from the very moment we enter this world, prior to every experience that shapes us one way or another. That special part of us can be shrouded sometimes, but it is always there, deep beneath. Let's be sure to be kind to ourselves today, especially during times of suffering. May our realisation that we are doing the best that we can in this moment of life, lift us towards actions that bring us, and others around us, joy.

August 20th

"You will never be happy if you continue to search for what happiness consists of. You will never live if you are looking for the meaning of life"

Albert Camus

Some scholars argue that 'happiness is action' and the Buddha famously proclaimed, "There is no path to happiness. Happiness is the path". But what do these words actually mean? I guess these statements suggest that you don't get to a certain level of wealth, or number of friends, or go to a certain place to 'become happy'. As happiness is a state of mind that can be experienced by all, it is to be interwoven into our sense of self every day. We must therefore find opportunities in our daily life to create happiness, where we are, as we are, today.

August 21st

"Your time is limited, so don't waste it living someone else's life. Don't be trapped by dogma – which is living with the results of other people's thinking. Don't let the noise of others' opinions drown out your own inner voice. And most important, have the courage to follow your heart and intuition"

Steve Jobs

The most important thing when bringing about your greater happiness may be learning to be kind to yourself, as if you cannot find true respect for who you are, then you cannot hear what is in your heart. True self-development is not self-denial; it is self-reformation. Today, let's take the energy we usually use for negative destructive functions, such as complaint about circumstances, and redirect that same energy towards positive aims.

August 22nd

"To know even one life has breathed easier because you have lived. This is to have succeeded"

Ralph Waldo Emerson

To remember this – to think this, to believe this – is the antidote to our feelings of powerlessness, uselessness and of apathy. Let's do this. Let's make a difference. In the queue at the supermarket through a naturally sparked conversation. In overcoming our difficulties to inspire others, and in the long-term paths we take in order to help others as we voyage on our own journey.

August 23rd

"Always turn a negative situation into a positive situation"

Michael Jordan

The simplicity of the quote may play down how possible and important this is. When we change something within, our same difficulty, becomes an opportunity. An opportunity to show our strength, to prove to ourselves we can do it, even if it means just pushing on and getting through it a day at a time. We can look back on a negative situation and see that along with the courage we expressed as we challenged it helped us in some way. Regrettably, the misfortune has a habit of obscuring from us the doors we must open, as we see only the doors it has firmly shut. Keep going ever open-minded today.

August 24th

"Action is the foundational key to all success"

Pablo Picasso

Action can change a situation, moving it in a completely unexpected direction. But sometimes it is so difficult to take such action because we are locked in feelings of disconnection and doubt. Let us break free from our doubt today, in the full knowledge that our brilliance is yet to come, and what is required of us right from the word go, is resilience, and consistent small and measurable steps to grow and fight our way forward, day by day.

August 25th

"The battles that count aren't the ones for gold medals. The struggles within yourself – the invisible, inevitable battles inside all of us – that's where it's at"

Jesse Owens.

Owens has an incredible insight here. We have external goals of course, but they ultimately matter only because of our inner life, our self-growth, our self-liberation. Today and everyday, let's strive positively and compassionately to better our life from yesterday to today so that our inner development, our foundation, grows and grows in strength too.

August 26th

"Great ideas spring not so much from noble intelligence as from noble feeling"

Fyodor Dostoevsky

If today is difficult, let's use our suffering by turning it into a rich empathy for the others around us who may be facing difficulties. We can become strong again and in turn inspire them, day by day. If today brings us joy, then from noble feeling, let's spread that light to others, through thoughts, words and actions that are from the heart.

August 27th

"Don't judge each day by the harvest you reap but by the seeds that you plant"

Robert Louis Stevenson

Whilst a farmer cannot see a farm full of crops in front of her, she still sows the seeds ready for a harvest to come, gaining fulfilment in the act of sowing, of planting. Based on our experience, we know that our hard work each day, and our efforts for others, will reap benefits for us in due course. Thus we too should gain great fulfilment from our initial actions – not just their effects.

August 28th

"I have learned that people will forget what you have said, people will forget what you did, but people will never forget how you made them feel"

Maya Angelou

We can't fail but make a difference to this world. All of our actions, no matter how small, change the world, literally, philosophically, scientifically – the key is just whether we make a positive difference or a negative difference, no matter how small or seismic the difference. Here's an example. Say we send a sincere message of kindness to a friend and it lifts them when they are having a bad day. In world x, they are having a bad day. In world x + kind message, they are having a bad day, then receive support from you and are lifted slightly in their heart. It doesn't matter how slightly – the world HAS changed. Their world has changed and you have changed it. Don't forget this today.

August 29th

"Too often we underestimate the power of a touch, a smile, a kind word, a listening ear, an honest compliment, or the smallest act of caring, all of which have the potential to turn a life around"

Leo Buscaglia

How do we feel when we are smiled at, when kind words are uttered to us, or we are truly heard out, listened to without judgement before encouraging words are offered? We feel good, positive, sometimes great and sometimes this goes with us into the rest of the day, or even beyond. We don't need positive psychology to confirm this, we know it so well. Let's do this, let's be this, let's live this today through the decisions and actions we engage in while we are with others.

August 30th

"I have been impressed with the urgency of doing. Knowing is not enough; we must apply. Being willing is not enough; we must do"

Leonardo da Vinci

I agree wholeheartedly that taking a view on an issue or an event in our life, or the lives of others, is not enough. Not enough to make a difference, and not enough to bring us lasting happiness. Thus as da Vinci says, every day we must move from virtue signalling to actually enacting change for ourselves and others. The actions we take can be small and manageable yet still tangible. This is the way to true fulfilment; as our actions match our minds, we are our true selves.

August 31st

"If you have a positive attitude and constantly strive to give your best effort, eventually you will overcome your immediate problems and find you are ready for greater challenges"

Pat Riley

The Bodhisattva way of Mahayana Buddhism, certainly from the perspective of Nichiren Buddhism, is metaphorically to delay one's own enlightenment and stay here engaged in this Saha world, or delusion, suffering, and desire, with the rest of humanity. There are two reasons for this: one, we cannot become truly happy without bringing others to see their happiness too (for we are all interconnected); and two, it is actually from the very earthly desires and sufferings of our lives, that we become happy, as we vow to grow and overcome adversity. Please know today that your suffering goes hand in hand with your victories too. Please don't give up, and, with inner strength, keep going one step at a time.

September 1st

"A successful person is one who can lay a firm foundation with the bricks that others throw at him or her"

David Brinkley

Sometimes we can read these quotes and feel that we are not this person, we cannot build from the bricks thrown at us, because they knock us down for so long, and are so debilitating. Really though, when one perseveres and continues, we don't realise that with the passage of time our growth comes out of the problem to become the mortar to piece together that which the suffering has taught us in our heart. Let's build from this, a castle of peace and empathy in our hearts, ever ready for our next challenge, to engage with courage what today will bring.

September 2nd

"The most exhausting thing in life is being insincere"

Anne Morrow Lindbergh

As a practitioner in education, I have this quote up in my classroom. The problem is, we don't know who we are, because we are consumed by social comparisons, both offline and online. I guess staying true to yourself means holding back for a second and, with sincere respect for the other person, saying what you mean. I guess it means taking the time to feel and record your aspirations and work towards them with integrity, dignity and empathy for others. Whatever it means to you, start today to steer away from following a homogeneous crowd, and bring who you are to the table, with deep respect for others, who are fully entitled to their individuality too.

September 3rd

"There is only one corner of the universe you can be certain of improving, and that's your own self"

Aldous Huxley

Life is about continually striving to improve ourselves, but in an organic, natural and day by day, small action by small action, sort of way. It's about doing it, not overdoing it. Let's not exhaust ourselves in constantly striving for personal change, yet let's slowly but surely grow and help others to be happier too. We can make a difference, we can't be static, everything is always changing and in a state of flux, from the galaxies to quantum particles. So let's change in the direction we wish to, starting from today.

September 4th

"Nothing in life is to be feared, it is only to be understood. Now is the time to understand more, so that we may fear less"

Marie Curie

When we are facing adversity at some point today, a struggle, an obstacle, if we can declare this obstacle is happening, then we can grow and learn. The issue is, it isn't until we overcome whatever is, however small or big, however internal or external the battle, that we can know what it will teach us, or, how much we will grow in strength until the battle is won. So that's where faith comes in, in oneself and in some fairly universal laws; overcoming the issue, will a be victory, will bring joy. We know it intellectually, but if we can begin to believe in our hearts, they can give just the right amount of courage to carry on.

September 5th

"Every moment and every event of every man's life on earth plants something in his soul"

Thomas Merton

The amazing thing is that whilst every action of ours is gradually and inconspicuously shaping our lives for the years to come, we cannot see the results as they will not manifest until much later. Just as the farmer who prepares her field cannot see the harvest, we cannot know the effects of the causes we are currently making. All we can do is ensure that we make positive causes, creatively contributing to our happiness and the happiness of others. Let's create some positive causes in our lives, starting from today.

September 6th

"This is the highest wisdom that I own; freedom and life are earned by those alone who conquer them each day anew"

Johann Wolfgang von Goethe

September brings a new start for all those who belong to an educational institution. I think that this sharpens the tools of self-renewal so that they become fully engaged. It is however my sincere belief that to begin this self-renewal every day, is to live a dynamic life in which we cannot fail to create value for ourselves and others. Let's renew who we are today, from this moment on, taking the action we need today to move forward and continue our personal stories.

September 7th

"I, not events, have the power to make me happy or unhappy today. I can choose which it shall be. Yesterday is dead, tomorrow hasn't arrived yet. I have just one day, today, and I'm going to be happy in it"

Groucho Marx

Whilst this is by no means possible to do, each and every day, there is a boldness in starting the day by saying, "today, I'm going to be happy". Look for happiness in the day, for opportunities in it, for opportunities to be human, to connect with others and be true to who you are. Let's approach today with self-belief and the expectation that today will be a day of value, a day we can value in the way we face it head on, with self-belief and a little smile that says keep going.

September 8th

"Success is to be measured not so much by the position that one has reached in life as by the obstacles which he has overcome"

Booker T. Washington

You can do it. You really do have boundless potential and strength to keep going. Keep working hard and you will get there. And remember, the hard work itself is an achievement, as it shows you are the protagonist in your life, taking the lead and initiative in shaping your future and overcoming obstacles in your path. As you're engaged in all that life has to offer today, please think to yourself, "the very fact that I am continuing on the face of this obstacle, means it has not defeated me and thus I have already begun to win over it in my heart".

September 9th

"Human greatness does not lie in wealth or power, but in character and goodness. People are just people, and all people have faults and shortcomings, but all of us are born with a basic goodness"

Anne Frank

As I tend to say with quotes from Anne Frank, she has profound insight. Sometimes amongst the whirlwind of suffering around us, wisdom lands like a butterfly on our shoulders. Frank sees to the heart of human goodness, in a time of immense human depravity. Let's apply her message today, reminding ourselves, with the kindness of a friend, we all have our faults, our shortcomings, so let's proceed today with the basic goodness that lies deep in our hearts, intent on creating value for those around us and for ourselves.

September 10th

"It's not only moving that creates new starting points. Sometimes all it takes is a subtle shift in perspective, an opening of the mind, an intentional pause and reset, or a new route to start to see new options and new possibilities"

Kristin Armstrong

To keep moving is to fall in line with the behaviour of the universe, at the microcosm of our lives; it is to be in sync with all things; it is to progress and become our future selves. Should we be struggling to keep going, struggling to change something fundamental, let's use our pauses, our rest breaks, our moments with others we trust or alone, as opportunities to reflect on what action we can take. Today, let's begin to reach out to others to help us shift our perspective from that which we cannot do, to that which we can.

September 11th

"One of the greatest discoveries a person makes, one of their great surprises, is to find they can do what they were afraid they couldn't do"

Henry Ford

At the end of a long road you do get that realisation that you've done it. In the midst of deep struggle, when we just keep going and don't give up, we may have the realisation, 'I'm doing it!' When some adversity rears its head, let's don the armour of courage, using our past successes as a cause to believe that we can do it – that we will do it – so that we can actually enjoy the challenge of striving to win, with a courage that overcomes our self-doubt.

September 12th

"Many raging fires are quenched by a single shower of rain, and many evil forces are vanquished by a single great truth"

Nichiren Daishonin

There is no simple way to put out the fire of the fears in our heart. Instead we must not be dismissive of our fears, fighting desperately to eradicate them. We first need to listen to them, commune with them internally, and wait to hear what it is they are trying to tell us. If we can listen to the message behind our fears, taking that message seriously, we can act to mitigate the concerns, deeply respecting the part of us that has held such fears for as many years as we have had them. This act of deep respect may lead to changes we had never conceived possible before.

September 13th

"There is no way to happiness, happiness is the way"

Thich Nhat Hanh

I genuinely believe that as much satisfaction can be derived from how we approach something, our attitude, as that which we have approached. That said, it means, our approach to our job, studies, family, hobbies, contributes as much to our satisfaction and fulfilment as what job or course we are doing. There are times, of course, when a change of direction is necessary, healthy and right. The same is true of life then. Nonetheless, how we live is just as important as what we've got. Let's live out our days with the view that we can add meaning and happiness where we are, as we are. Let's look for opportunities to create happiness right here, right now, for ourselves and others, whatever the circumstances.

September 14th

"Friendship is love without his wings!"

Lord Byron

If we have good people in our life, let's keep such good people close to our chest, close to heart, continuing to develop our connections. If we find this lacking in our lives, let's take a step today towards forming such connections with those we come into contact with, so we can sincerely develop heart-to-heart bonds. In short, let's make sure we are always there when one needs the support of another. And when it is our heart that needs love without wings, let's ask sincerely for this invaluable support.

September 15th

"In times of crisis, people reach out for meaning. Meaning is strength. Our survival may depend on our seeking and finding it"

Viktor Frankl

In his writings Viktor Frankl, who survived the horrors of four concentration camps, quotes the writing of Friedrich Nietzsche who states, "He who has a why to live for can bear almost any how". Whatever you are facing today – however big, small, surmountable, insurmountable – let there be meaning there, let there be value you are creating by the way you positively and resiliently keep going, gaining courage, conviction and inspiring others along the way.

September 16th

"When one door closes, another opens, but often we look so long at the closed door that we do not see the one that has been opened for us"

Helen Keller

Helen Keller, the first blind-deaf person to receive a degree, worked tirelessly alongside her incredible teacher, Anne Sullivan, to become an inspiration to so many today. She knew what she could not do, and yet sought with all her being for the doors that were open to her, however stiff they were. In our lives, which are so unique and so different in their content and character, we need to keep our hearts open when doors close, and believe in ourselves to turn positively towards that which we can do, that which awaits us, to create positive value there.

September 17th

"This too shall pass"

Persian Proverb

Though the exact origin of this phrase is unknown, its truth is universal. It is a truth that gives us hope, keeps us going and can even persuade us to see ourselves as the protagonist in our situation, who can bring hope to others.

September 18th

"I'll never be able to do that." The power of the entire universe is inherent in our lives. When we firmly decide, "I can do it!" we can break through the walls of self-imposed limitations"

Daisaku Ikeda

Whilst we move in the UK towards more autumnal weather, I hope that the earlier sunsets are accompanied by the rich tapestry of colour that autumn has to offer. May this quote lift you as we move towards the part of the year that can become more difficult sometimes internally. Faith is to begin, even when one does not know where the road reads. Whatever you wish to change, to move, to shift, to create, to become – gain strength in everything you have done until now; begin with a smile in your heart today.

September 19th

"In order to carry a positive action we must develop here a positive vision."

Dalai Lama

Where do we get this positive vision from? It does depend on your personal faith. If you are a theist, it may come from prayer to and with God. If you are a Buddhist, it may be prayer, a vow of intention, in one's own heart. And if you are a humanist/atheist, you may find your own methods, drawing out, visualising, or talking it through with others. Perhaps secular meditation may allow you to breathe into the thoughts beneath your worries and concern. However you do it, part of breaking through is finding faith in a longer-term vision of what you want to change, or see come to fruition, in your life and the lives of others. Let's begin this vision today, moving towards it in our hearts each day.

September 20th

"An arrogant person considers himself perfect. This is the chief harm of arrogance. It interferes with a person's main task in life – becoming a better person"

Leo Tolstoy

Whilst incredibly subjective, I really think this task of becoming a 'better person' is related to understanding the plight of others and taking some action to alleviate it. I think that if people work at this on a one-to-one basis, we will gradually get a better world. When I first committed this to writing, I had recently shared a dialogue with a homeless man in the city of Norwich, UK. He and his dog were sitting there as I left the car park, so I sat down for a few minutes, just for a chat, to show I saw him as a person, as a dignified human being; we had a nice chat. Then on my way back from the meeting I saw a couple who were sitting down having a chat with him too. This made me realise it takes very little effort at times, from relatively few people, to improve this world. It just takes a little time each day to appreciate each other's dignity. The more of us that show this compassion, the better we become.

September 21st

"Those who see the cosmic perspective as a depressing outlook, they really need to reassess how they think about the world. Because when I look up in the universe, I know I'm small but I'm also big. I'm big because I'm connected to the universe, and the universe is connected to me"

Neil deGrasse Tyson

The renowned American Astrophysicist has hit the nail on the head: when we really think about it, we and everything around us, on a quantum level, are fundamentally made of the same stuff; i.e. the building blocks of the universe are in all things. Not only this, but Pauli's exclusion principle alludes to the fact that if we change the quantum state of one particle in a particular way, then all other particles in the system (the universe) must change too. As we are made of these incredible interconnected universal building blocks, let's believe in our power to change things around us today, remembering how all that which is around us is connected to us on a deep level.

September 22nd

"Don't be satisfied with stories, how things have gone for others. Unfold your own myth"

Jalal ad-Din Muhammad Rumi

Rumi speaks from the 13th Century to us right now. We are incredibly affected by and caught up in the stories of others. We cannot go through one day without comparing ourselves in one way or another to the lives of people we know or to those we see on our screens. It is clear that comparison brings unhappiness and most importantly as Rumi suggests, it stops us from making great changes in our own lives; it stops us from becoming who we wish to become in our hearts, as we lose spiritual insight to that which matters most to us. Let's begin where we are today, fully ready and even excited about the challenge of beginning to unlock our myth one day at a time.

September 23rd

"He has achieved success who has lived well, laughed often and loved much; who has gained the respect of intelligent men and the love of little children; who has filled his niche and accomplished his task; who has left the world better than he found it, whether by an improved poppy, a perfect poem, or a rescued soul"

Bessie A. Stanley

Let's not overcomplicate how amazing we can be, what incredible potential we have, bogging it down with doubt and deprecation. It is true, as Stanley says, that success in life is a measure, not of wealth or fame, but of what we leave behind. Let our legacy, however small, however personal, be beautiful at heart, and lift others in some way. May we leave a truth that can shelter others; may we leave this world knowing that we appreciated others around us, lifted them, and – through our positive actions – left the world a little better.

September 24th

"Contentment is the only real wealth"

Alfred Nobel

To be happier we have to focus on what we have, whilst still working for that which we have not. We begin by focussing on the good inside ourselves and others, whilst aiming too to help develop the negatives. A shift of momentum on what we can change, rather than that which we can't. Whilst it is completely fair to sit there and say, 'but I can't change my thinking', one can definitely begin to catch oneself doing the unproductive and negative internal dialogue that can plague our minds, and however unnaturally at first, begin one day at a time to switch to a more positive angle. Through redirecting these thoughts, with a smile, today and on to tomorrow we will, after a few weeks or so, start to see a move towardsa more positive take on situations. Let's begin this today.

September 25th

"Let your mind alone, and see what happens"

Virgil Thomson

From my study of philosophy and my personal readings of some of the existentialists, if you want to live a life where you feel fully alive, you need to get on with living it. Thinking about your purpose often diminishes it, as you go around in circles; I believe this is because it is impossible to truly understand your purpose by intellect alone. I could think intellectually about my view that life has meaning when you contribute towards the happiness of yourself and others, until the cows come home, but mere contemplation reduces how special it is to live like this, to a series of words. Instead, by living out our lives in a truly contributive way, we can feel the very meaning of life pulsing through our sense of self, hour by hour, day by day; we can feel it in our hearts that our actions truly make a difference. Let's live fully with this spirit of purpose.

September 26th

"It takes a long time to become young"

Pablo Picasso

As a young child, one often lives in the moment, free of worry and concern. When we grow up we can then spend our adult lives developing the wisdom and courage to get back to that feeling of experiencing the here and now. The person I look up to that embodies this youthful spirit, is a man in his 90s named Daisaku Ikeda; a man who has fought his whole life for peace, and strived continuously for the happiness of others. He has done this until this late age precisely because he maintains that youthful freedom of spirit, yet has the wisdom of a life long-lived to utilise it. Let's strive to live with that youthful ease of vitality in spirit, with the wisdom to freely take action for the happiness of ourselves and others.

September 27th

"Listening is a positive act: you have to put yourself out to do it"

David Hockney

We think listening is the most natural thing in the world but it really does take incredible effort to embrace what someone is saying wholeheartedly with non-judgemental understanding. I naturally can be very poor at listening as my mind gets sidetracked by other thoughts. I have had to work on this, and for me there is one clear answer, which is easy to understand yet difficult to implement consistently, because of our ego. The answer is empathy. If we truly care about how the person speaking is thinking and feeling, it can the conversation so we can truly connect. Let's really care for the life of the other person who has chosen us to open up to today.

September 28th

"The secret to happiness is freedom... And the secret to freedom is courage"

Thucydides

Let's have the courage today to win where we are, as we are, regardless of our fear, and our strongest opponent, our doubt. We may be doubting we can do it, but let's push on. We may be fearful of the outcome, but let's push on. We can, by virtue of continuing, open the door to a rising self-belief, a confidence that eventually empowers us as we get ever closer to making the progress we seek.

September 29th

"Great things are done when men and mountains meet"

William Blake

The greater the climb, the greater the effort, the greater the achievement. What great things and difficult things have we achieved or accomplished in our lives to date? When we look back at what we are most proud of, we find that these accomplishments, personal or otherwise, were more often than not achieved through sheer grit and determination. Let's remember this in the course of our current difficulties and continue with ever greater courage in full knowledge of how proud we will be when we get through them.

September 30th

"Language is the armory of the human mind, and at once contains the trophies of its past and the weapons of its future conquests"

Samuel Taylor Coleridge

Words can heal, words can harm, and words can reveal to others, our genuine concern for their wellbeing. By extension, the right words, in the right way, at the right time, can change somebody else's life. Let's use our words wisely with the intent to lift others, to show we care, and to speak out with courage against injustice when we see it.

October 1st

"This is my simple religion. There is no need for temples; no need for complicated philosophy. Our own brain, our own heart is our temple; the philosophy is kindness"

The Dalai Lama

The people I look up to, I ultimately look up to because of their actions. Yes what Dr King, Gandhi, Frank, Mandela, Keller, Frankl, Angelou and countless others say is profound, but it is only so incredibly meaningful because they lived by their words. Let's aim to live true to our beliefs and our words, picking ourselves back up without judgement and redoubling our efforts should we fall short of such courage. Today lets act towards ourselves and others in a way that is truly kind, a way that accords with who we wish to be.

October 2nd

"Nothing wilts faster than laurels that have been rested upon"

Percy Bysshe Shelley

Shelley makes the incredibly profound point that to not take some action each day for our happiness and the happiness of others around us, is to regress. All things are changing at each moment from the smallest subatomic particle to the largest celestial body, therefore we are no different. Should we wish to be truly happy, we must take action each day to discover how incredible we can be and not be put off taking such action whilst our self esteem wilts.

October 3rd

"When I thought I couldn't go on, I forced myself to keep going. My success is based on persistence, not luck"

Estée Lauder

In a physical struggle to push on and become the best athlete one can be, there can be a pain barrier to push through, to continue through, to overcome and get out the other side and through this success the athlete becomes stronger and achieves their personal best. In our own lives, which are a form of spiritual gym – a continual spiritual training – there are moments too in our endeavours and struggles, whether chosen or not, that if we can just galvanise enough spiritual strength to continue through then on the other side lies success; the opportunity to look and realise how very much we have overcome, how incredibly strong we can be. Let's not give up today and keep going in the knowledge that in doing so we are expressing incredible spiritual strength.

October 4th

"My mission in life is not merely to survive, but to thrive; and to do so with some passion, some compassion, some humor, and some style"

Maya Angelou

To thrive is to fight to overcome great adversity. To meet it with courage and hope in equal measure. Coping is all we can do sometimes, but when we begin to adopt an attitude of fearlessness, we begin to overcome our obstacles with humour and style, beginning to embrace life as a journey, not a destination.

October 5th

"I've learned that fear limits you and your vision. It serves as blinders to what may be just a few steps down the road for you. The journey is valuable, but believing in your talents, your abilities, and your self-worth can empower you to walk down an even brighter path. Transforming fear into freedom – how great is that?"

Soledad O'Brien

Sometimes, to overcome fear we not only need to dig in and use our inner determination, but we also need to come back to and ask for sincere support from those we trust, whether they be friends, or family members – biological or adopted. However we develop, grow and ensure our own self-belief, let's take the action we need to, to ensure we can believe in our talent to overcome and transform the struggles we find ourselves engaged in today.

October 6th

"Growth is painful. Change is painful. But, nothing is as painful as staying stuck where you do not belong"

N. R. Narayana Murthy

Whatever struggles we are facing let's take the time and space where possible to have moments of reflection and rest – listening to the toll such difficulties take on our minds and bodies. However small such moments of self-care may be, I deeply hope they can help us to continue on whatever personal journey we find ourselves on today.

October 7th

"The essence of philosophy is that a man should so live that his happiness shall depend as little as possible on external things"

Epictetus

To take control of our happiness is to look for it less and less outside of oneself. Societally we look to wealth, status, fame and other individuals as routes to becoming happy. This is understandable because these things do affect our happiness, however to 'rely' or 'depend on' them for our happiness can cause us further suffering, as we do not have control over how these variables in our life change given the passage of time. Therefore to become truly happy we need to view ourselves as separate entities to our outside influences, very much affected by them, but empowered by the understanding, that we ourselves can take responsibility for enhancing and building a happy self, from this moment on, through the small, consistent and concerted actions over time, regardless of the positive or negative influences we are currently challenged by.

October 8th

"An invasion of armies can be resisted, but not an idea whose time has come"

Victor Hugo

Hugo's take on this theme of ideas enduring, is that once an incredible idea has lit the minds of people in society to the point in which they believe it to be possible to see such change, this flame cannot be diminished should enough people possess the vigour and courage to pursue it. May the idea that we matter, that we are just as special as everyone else, that we can make a difference, light our minds. May the idea that we have the inner strength and courage we require to rise up to meet all our obstacles be ever present in our hearts.

October 9th

"Problems are not the problem; coping is the problem"

Virginia Satir

There is a danger of lifting quotes from the context in which they appear. This is not about blaming oneself when we cannot cope, cannot go on. What this quote is alluding to is that when we realise that the bigger our problems, the stronger we have to hold on, the deeper we have to dig. To dig deep, to hold on, implies we need to bring forth courage, strength and prove to ourselves how amazing we can really be. Problems then do not solely imply crisis, they provide us with opportunity too. In battling our difficulties we can find happiness in winning over them, either in eradicating the problem itself, or in our all out efforts to grow around it. We still experience the same suffering and difficulty of course but this psychological shift allows us to consider that we may experience the exhilaration and empowerment that comes as we begin to challenge our circumstances too.

October 10th

"Generosity is giving more than you can, and pride is taking less than you need"

Khalil Gibran

Let's keep up a genuine, sincere and open communication so that we too can ask what we need of others, with respect, when the time is right. Opening our connections has the long-term effect of enhancing our wellbeing. It also enables us to support others in whatever way we can when they most need it, affirming our humanity, self-worth and dignity, as well as their inherent worth too. Let's live the word humanity through our own actions and our connections as we strive to reach out to others.

October 11th

"This is the real secret of life – to be completely engaged with what you are doing in the here and now. And instead of calling it work, realize it is play"

Alan Watts

To engage in the moment fully, is to experience meaning. Let's engage in all our activities with the view that each and every one will shape who we are, and who we can be. Regardless of the future yet to come, whether it be suffering, joy or any emotion in between, let us be there in the moment, let us grow.

October 12th

"Service to others is the rent you pay for your room here on earth"

Muhammad Ali

Numerous studies since the advent of positive psychology in the 1990s point to the benefits of helping others, some stating that an action of an altruistic nature for someone else can benefit the person who acts in this way with a positive feeling for up to four days later. True happiness is when we become happy alongside others. Let our service to others be manageable, consider our own interests and needs and also be sustainable. However small our actions for others, let us be proud in each and every action that can lift people around us.

October 13th

"Happiness in intelligent people is the rarest thing I know"

Ernest Hemingway

Intelligence interrupts true happiness as our inner reflection interprets and analyses that which is best experienced in the moment. Often this indistinct inner-self concentrates on how to improve a past that is unchangeable and how to change a future that is yet to be. Thus to take action in the present from one moment to enjoy what there is to enjoy, to be the protagonist in our difficulties and to organically become who we wish to be.

October 14th

"A strong, positive self-image is the best possible preparation for success"

Joyce Brothers

Believe in yourself; believe in your capacity to make a difference, your ability to change, your potential for resilience in the face of adversity. If we can adopt this self-image, whilst enlisting the kindness and support of others, we will begin to face each day of our lives as empowered agents with respsonsibility for the self-reformation and value creation we seek.

October 15th

"It is one of the most beautiful compensations of this life that no man can sincerely try to help another without helping himself"

Ralph Waldo Emerson

The key to solving a problem or making your way through an impasse is to see it differently. How might overcoming this problem help you grow? How might facing it head-on inspire and support others? How might you be able to help other people with a similar problem once you overcome it? What qualities are you developing as you resiliently face your challenges? What can you learn with each difficulty you face – about yourself or others? Keep going day by day, and you will grow, inspiring others in the process who see hope too. Never give up and always believe in your innate potential!

October 16th

"Adopting the right attitude can convert a negative stress into a positive one"

Hans Selye

Whilst some of the challenges of our lives are huge and seem insurmountable, many of our day-to-day stresses and difficulties are possible to face in one of two ways: one, with a positive disposition connected to our role in changing the situation, or two, a negative disposition concerned with how the situation arose. The quicker we can focus on creating a solution, the quicker we can become positive about the actions we are taking; as we focus on the bit we can change, the less and less we will focuss on that which we cannot. In those day-to-day difficulties, let's begin to shine a little light on a way forward for us and those around us.

October 17th

"A great man is a torch in the darkness, a beacon in superstition's night, an inspiration and a prophecy"

Robert Green Ingersoll

With such horror occurring in the world we live in, we can only redouble our efforts to show kindness to those lives we personally come into contact with each day. Where there is darkness, we can exemplify light. To create value wherever we go and for whoever we speak to, treating the person in front of us with deep respect, is to become a beacon of hope for others to see, encouraging them that they too can make a positive difference, day by day. Please believe in our capacity to do this, one action at a time.

October 18th

"In essence, if we want to direct our lives, we must take control of our consistent actions. It's not what we do once in a while that shapes our lives, but what we do consistently"

Anthony Robbins

Small changes that we can stick to have such a profound effect on our wellbeing and happiness. If these changes are governed by the five causes of happiness that have been proven by social research – expressing our gratitude, manageable altruistic actions, being present in the moment (mindful living), engaging in our community and focussing on our self-worth – our wellbeing will be affected in a positive way.

October 19th

"Although the world is full of suffering, it is also full of the overcoming of it"

Helen Keller

Let's rise to our challenges. The bigger they get, the stronger we respond in spirit to meet them, and thus we grow each time they come to greet us. We can overcome our difficulties, we can show the greatness of the human spirit, of our spirit, by facing our circumstances with the disposition that the hard work to overcome them has already begun. Let's rise positively today to engage fully in what life has to offer, as we are.

October 20th

"Enough words have been exchanged; now at last let me see some deeds!"

Johann Wolfgang von Goethe

Taking action every day for our happiness and the happiness of others is a sure-fire way to feel alive, to feel like we matter. We cannot seize the moment until we are fully committed to our belief in change, thus we must first search our hearts for that which moves us, that which matters to us, and then begin to take steps in that direction, through our actions from this day forward.

October 21st

> **"No one can better bask in summer's balm than those who have endured winter's bite. Similarly, it is those who have suffered through life's darkest hours who are able to truly savour the bright dawn of happiness. The person who has transformed the worst of fate into the best of fortune is life's champion"**
>
> Daisaku Ikeda

I know some of you reading this will have faced the bitterest of suffering in the past, and some of you will be facing some deep difficulties right now. Please know that no one can take away how we choose to react to our suffering, and thus, how we choose to act when we face deep hardship; it is an opportunity to show who we really are. It is our chance to exhibit our self-worth and rise up, creating value from where we are right now, hour by hour, day by day. My deepest prayer is that we find the strength to rise up in the face of our difficulties today.

October 22nd

"Sometimes I wish that I could go into a time machine right now and just look at my self and say, 'Calm down. Things are gonna be fine. Things are gonna be all great. Just relax'"

Tristan Wilds

How true is this for so many of our ventures and the stresses they bring? Today, let's try to face our difficulties head on, as if we have experienced them already before and won. Let's approach our difficulties with the confidence that we can create value from each struggle, and in doing so begin to unleash our greater qualities of resilience and courage.

October 23rd

"I have always been delighted at the prospect of a new day, a fresh try, one more start, with perhaps a bit of magic waiting somewhere behind the morning"

J. B. Priestley

Here's to a new day. With everything learnt from times foregone; the ups, the downs, the successes and mistakes, let's take on the opportunities that today brings with a smile and beautiful inner strength that comes from the belief in our potential in each moment.

October 24th

"Happiness is when what you think, what you say, and what you do are in harmony"

Mahatma Gandhi

We can give our life meaning like we can give a canvas colour. It's the unique composition of our choices that's important. To understand our uniqueness, or least to come closer to what it feels like to live exactly as we believe we should live, is to begin living true to ourselves and slowly reap the benefit of being at ease with who we are, wherever we are.

October 25th

"This above all; to thine own self be true"

William Shakespeare

I really believe a lot of our inner stress and anxiety is largely reduced when we begin to live a life of genuine substance, a life in which we act in a way that is, and take decisions that are, truly representative of who we are and who we want to be. With great respect for others, let's act in accord with our most sincere beliefs of dignity, respect and compassion in order to create a self of great integrity, a self we can learn to love, accept and embrace for our wellbeing and the wellbeing of others around us.

October 26th

"You can find peace amidst the storms that threaten you"

Joseph B. Wirthlin

And this peace arrives at the moment of clarity when we go from thinking to fully believing, "I'm going to get through this". To know we are going to be OK is not enough, the sooner we can feel that we have the strength to survive the storm, the better. This is why we must support each other, why we must be there for each other. Let's use our unlimited potential to stand strong together, and continue to grow as we turn the storms of our lives into an opportunity to prove we have the mettle we didn't know we even possessed.

October 27th

"Life is what we make it, always has been, always will be"

Grandma Moses

Today and from now on, we as the protagonists can step forward on our ever continuing journeys of change. In the tough times we must be believe in change, and in the good times and everything in between, we continue to lead that change. We are ever becoming, ever growing, life creating. How very special it is, that the direction of travel is in our very hands.

October 28th

"Hope is like the sun, which, as we journey toward it, casts the shadow of our burden behind us"

Samuel Smiles

Whatever hope we hold in our situation, whether it be to overcome it, transform it, change it, or even win in the face of it, or just to create something of positive value within the darkness that tries to consume us; please continue with hope in your heart and the belief that we can shine bright enough to illuminate those around us – if we stay committed to not giving up, one day at a time.

October 29th

"You cannot live without enemies. And the fact of the matter is, the more upright you live, the more enemies you will have"

Leo Tolstoy

This quote from Tolstoy is so important, but we may need to adapt the word enemy to fully grasp it in the 21st Century. When we choose to stand up, to advance our lives, we are going to be judged. People may judge us as false, as fake, perhaps they will comment through a subconscious jealousy that we shaking off the chains of karma to become authentically ourselves. When we are sincere in our convictions we grow in our ability to say something assertively that needs to be said to help someone struggling, and this again invites judgement, comment and criticism. One way to keep moving forwards is to be sincere and keep growing when we face this, by remembering that we will judged either way. There is no escape from judgement, and sometimes when it is oppositional it actually clarifies the good we are doing.

October 30th

"Everything beautiful has a mark of eternity"

Simone Weil

Our actions have ripple effects, as described in Lorenz's butterfly effect theory – we cannot deny that what we do changes the course of eternity. This quote though, points to more than this knock-on effect of actions. It points instead to the special tranquillity that is found in sincerely experiencing a moment without judgement, concern and thought of the future or past. Let's experience little moments of eternity today, by being there in the moment, when alone and with the others we come into contact with today.

October 31st

"If you would take, you must first give, this is the beginning of intelligence"

Lao Tzu

If we understand what it is for someone to extend kindness to us, to know the assurance and acceptance it brings, then how can we fail to understand the effect our actions have on others when we do the same? On this basis, this knowledge, this wisdom, let's extend such kindness, however small our actions may seem, today. Never belittle the profound impact we can have on others around us.

November 1st

"The comfort zone is the great enemy to creativity; moving beyond it necessitates intuition, which in turn configures new perspectives and conquers fears"

Dan Stevens

Creativity is human behaviour at its purest. I think that when we direct our creativity into action, with a wish to benefit ourselves and others, our faith in ourselves gets the rejuvenation that is so regularly required to face our challenges head-on. So let's take a little action with this special intent today, ever able to see that we really can make a difference, where we are, as we are.

November 2nd

"I see my path, but I don't know where it leads. Not knowing where I'm going is what inspires me to travel it"

Rosalia de Castro

We don't know where our paths are leading and that is what makes life so daunting, yet so incredibly special. To move beyond our fear to awe, I believe, is to become engrossed in being the protagonist of the best future we can create for ourselves and those around us. Through living the most contributive life we can, in a way that also accords to and respects our own well-being, we can truly live in the present.

November 3rd

"I find hope in the darkest of days, and focus in the brightest. I do not judge the universe"

The Dalai Lama

I sincerely hope there is true brightness within our day today, that gains our focus for some time. Should today be a day of struggle, may hope lift us just enough to have the courage to face our difficulties head-on, with the belief that today we will create value exactly where we are, as we are. By continuing and by surprising ourselves with positivity, we can begin to galvanise ourselves in moments of darkness.

November 4th

"Do you not see how necessary a world of pains and troubles is to school an intelligence and make it a soul?"

John Keats

It might be one of the most difficult things in the world, but if we can learn to use our tenacity in facing difficulties to enable us to become happier as we overcome them, we become victors in life, ever with hope and inner belief in our hearts. Let's tenaciously push on in the face of the what life brings today.

November 5th

"We are all human beings, whatever our positions. If we open our hearts and speak with sincerity, we can communicate and touch others on the deepest level. World peace starts with trusts between one individual and another"

Daisaku Ikeda

We can have a huge influence on each other. We only have to think of the profoundly negative effect someone's unjust and disrespectful treatment of us can have on the way we feel for the rest of the day. So today, let's be sincere in our dialogues, with a genuine compassion for the happiness of others and a belief that that which we say and do does indeed make a profound difference to the thoughts and feelings of others.

November 6th

"One life is all we have and we live it as we believe in living it. But to sacrifice what you are and to live without belief, that is a fate more terrible than dying"

Joan of Arc

Let us believe in who we are, what touches us deeply, what strikes us as the most joyful. Let's pursue who we are, and shine as the person we wish to be, regardless of success in those matters of the heart. May we be full of pride in that which we continued to pursue and become, as we look back over the course of time.

November 7th

"I cannot even imagine where I would be today were it not for that handful of friends who have given me a heart full of joy. Let's face it, friends make life a lot more fun"

Charles R. Swindoll

May those around us multiply our joys and halve our troubles. May we continue to create and secure connections with others that will last a lifetime. May we continue to be there when those around us need a heart-to-heart, and have the strength to speak out when it is us who need to be supported. May we continue to find joy in the joy of others and together move forward in life with those around us.

November 8th

"If we take eternity to mean not infinite temporal duration but timelessness, then eternal life belongs to those who live in the present"

Ludwig Wittgenstein

Expressing the present moment as eternal may be philosophical or poetic but it helps us refocus our attitude to the here and now. As Sophocles says, "Fortune cannot aid those who do nothing". If we concentrate on the importance of each present moment that we become aware of today, we can set up more of these special moments in the future as we begin to establish more and more positive causes in our lives. We can also move away from any mistakes of the past by concentrating on all that we really have: the here and now.

November 9th

"If you don't like something, change it. If you can't change it, change your attitude"

Maya Angelou

Civil rights activist Angelou makes an important statement here, which is also echoed by Holocaust survivor and Psychologist Viktor Frankl, who says, "When we are no longer able to change a situation – we are challenged to change ourselves". But what do they and other commentators mean? I believe they allude to the following: to focus on a problem without a solution is to walk a path of despair, whereas to use this desire for change, and to direct it to action in our lives and the lives of others, in which we still can create value, is to live a truly admirable life of hope and determination.

November 10th

"Yesterday I was clever, so I wanted to change the world. Today I am wise, so I am changing myself"

Jalal ad-Din Muhammad Rumi

Rumi's insight is incredibly profound. Sometimes we forget that if we really do want to move people around us, and make a difference, it is a change in our hearts that is first needed. By continuing on our own personal journeys to become who we wish to be, and to act in accordance with what we believe, is to show others a path too. So today, let's build from where we are now, as ourselves and completely unique in who we are. Let's build from the ground up, with the tools we have, one step at a time.

November 11th

"Appreciation is a wonderful thing: It makes what is excellent in others belong to us as well"

Voltaire

Often we live in the midst of such a competitive culture, that the idea of 'you win and I win too' is quite alien to us. We assume our happiness comes from emerging from within the pack, to show how well we have done, constantly comparing ourselves to others. In doing so we feed our ego, unaware of the benefits one can harness from celebrating and appreciating the successes of each other on a regular basis. In social scientific studies, participants who express their gratitude in written and verbal form show increases in their happiness and wellbeing. Think how much more happiness we would create in our communities if we could really appreciate the successes and strengths of each other rising together to succeed in our lives and to meet our challenges head on; without comparisons, and with beautifully sincere praise.

November 12th

"Expect problems and eat them for breakfast"

Alfred A. Montapert

Please do not underestimate your ability to overcome problems. Your strength in adversity is only enhanced when you expect problems to arise. Problems to action, are like gravity to mass. Problems will come as direct evidence that we are moving forward in an area of our life, they are a testament that we are creating value for ourselves and others. As problems arise we can choose to view them as opportunities to turn around, opportunities to create happiness, as we begin to grow in strength and character in the face of them.

November 13th

"Happiness is a butterfly, which when pursued, is always just beyond your grasp, but which, if you will sit down quietly, may alight upon you"

Nathaniel Hawthorne

It is my sincere conviction that engaging in the struggles we are facing right now, winning over them with great courage and determination, is the strongest way to create the foundations of lasting happiness we seek. In challenging adversity we have to believe we can grow bigger than the problem itself. It's this sense of fulfilment that comes from the effort required to overcome our obstacles, and when we begin to adopt a lasting sense of who we can be, there is so much that we begin to achieve. The butterfly of happiness loves to settle on the shoulder of those weary from their victory over their struggles – absolute victory in life comes when we exhibit our wisdom and courage in the midst of adversity – often she decides to settle whilst we are still in the midst of our challenge, knowing in our heart that we've already won.

November 14th

"We cannot live better than in seeking to become better"

Socrates

Those of us who seek to live a good life are living a good life. Those of us who live as though our lives have great meaning, give our lives such meaning. Let's seek to become our better selves each day, picking ourselves up when we fall, learning when we fail, but ever moving towards our future selves on a journey of small but significant actions that we take each day, and in doing so we will reveal our greater selves along the way.

November 15th

"He who is not courageous enough to take risks will accomplish nothing in life"

Muhammad Ali

Ali is an inspiration to many, especially in his hard work, determination, and courageously staying true to his beliefs during times in which they were questioned by many. There is a beautiful authenticity to his actions of throwing his Olympic medal in the river after returning to segregation and refusing to fight in the horrific war in Vietnam for a country that wouldn't secure his rights. So he knew about courage. Courage doesn't mean you're not scared, but it does mean you believe that you're right to carry on, that you will get there in the end with the passage of time.

November 16th

"Start where you are. Use what you have. Do what you can"

Arthur Ashe

Please take great pride in creating your future from where you are right now. Every step we take in the direction of creating value, for ourselves and others, from exactly where we are right now, is proof that we ourselves can challenge and win. Challenging our situation with resilience and endurance is a celebration of the inner strength we already possess.

November 17th

"To see a world in a grain of sand and a heaven in a wild flower, hold infinity in the palm of your hand and eternity in an hour"

William Blake

I hope we experience a little bit of infinity today. May we, at some point in our day, be captivated by the moment. May it be a moment of inner clarity, or a mindfulness of what is going on around us. Either way, let's feel what it is to be human, and may these little moments of eternity rejuvenate our spirits as we continue on our personal journeys as the protagonists of our stories.

November 18th

"Death is more certain than the morrow, than night following day, than winter following summer. Why is it then that we prepare for the night and for the winter time, but do not prepare for death. We must prepare for death. But there is only one way to prepare for death – and that is to live well"

Leo Tolstoy

You may be surprised to read this quote in a book of encouragement, day by day, one day at a time. But let's focus on the sentiment expressed in the final line which asks us; to live well. Emerson, in another quote in this book – alludes that a life lived well is one in which we we leave the world a little better than we found it. This may be true, but why wait to consider the entirety of our lives when we begin to live more fully today. Let us feel inspired by Tolstoy's call to start living well – let us open ourselves to joy when the moment allows, and let us share this life with others, the ups and downs, creating value for ourselves and those around us as we go. This is to live well.

November 19th

"I don't think of all the misery, but of the beauty that still remains"

Anne Frank

And part of the beauty that remains is our ability to change our lives and the lives of others for the better. We cannot underestimate how much we can lift and how much we can enact positive change in our own lives. The key to the door of change is in not giving up each time we fall; to keep going means to continue to develop and grow, one action at a time.

November 20th

"Do not look for approval except for the consciousness of doing your best"

Andrew Carnegie

We are constantly looking for approval outside of ourselves for our actions. Until we truly judge our actions for the effort we put in and our sincere intent to improve the situation, we will not free ourselves from the shackles of a judgemental self. We have to keep growing in our strength of conviction that putting our all into what we believe to be right and worthy to be doing, is a life well lived. Let's concentrate on our intent today as we show the kindness of a friend of old in our judgements of ourselves.

November 21st

"When obstacles arise, you change your direction to reach your goal; you do not change your decision to get there"

Zig Ziglar

Whatever we are trying to do, achieve or overcome today, let us not give up. Let us keep going, changing tack, direction, perhaps even our strategy when necessary, and raising our efforts when we need to. Let our obstacles show us how much progress we are making so far, and may our resolve strengthen ever more in the face of that which life has in store for us today.

November 22nd

"I am not a saint, unless you think of a saint as a sinner who keeps on trying"

Nelson Mandela

If we are continually moving in the right direction, working to improve our faults, and if our intent is to be good and just, then we are already a good person in our hearts. Often people are hard on themselves, taking their flaws or lack of action to be unchangeable; fixed. This of course is untrue, and to always pick ourselves up each time we fail – to act as calmly, courageously or wisely as we would wish – is what really makes us great as human beings. So let's never give up and always keep going, and in our hearts we have already become the people we wish to be.

November 23rd

"It is easy to sit up and take notice, What is difficult is getting up and taking action"

Honore de Balzac

Our thoughts are subjective as they pertain only to us, the subject. No one else can access them. It is clear that we are much more than our thoughts; in truth we are also defined by our speech, actions, and our intent, our heart. The effect our words and actions have becomes profoundly objective in contrast, as they clearly exist beyond our own minds. Today, let's see our actions as an extension of who we are, as our objective way of making our mark on the world around us and never forget today, and every day, the profound effect we can make on others around us.

November 24th

"What sunshine is to flowers, smiles are to humanity. These are but trifles, to be sure; but scattered along life's pathway, the good they do is inconceivable"

Joseph Addison

I really do believe that the good we do for others, however small it be, has a profound effect, given enough to account for all future connected effects. I believe this chain of events, known as Lorenz's butterfly effect, has extraordinary implications when we multiply the causes we make by our, on average, 28000 days on earth. Our lives therefore really are incredibly profound! And should we choose to create value for ourselves and others along the way, I believe this will become crystal clear. So today, believing in the difference we can make, let's take the action we need to, for ourselves and for the people around us.

November 25th

"With realization of one's own potential and self-confidence in one's ability, one can build a better world"

The Dalai Lama

If we're suffering from lack of self-belief it is a catch 22. To see our greatness we need be able to make a difference, but to have the get up and go to make a difference we have to believe we can make it. How do we square this dilemma? Perhaps we can consult our memories of the times we have lifted people, made them smile and how that made us feel too. Please know that it is not about quantity, but quality. Let's enjoy the challenge of creating some positive effects around us, regardless of the quantity of the actions we are able to take today.

November 26th

"Time is more valuable than money. You can get more money but you cannot get more time"

Jim Rohn

I think this unveils the hidden truth that a big part of being happy is, as Tolstoy argues, to live the years, not count them. To live wholeheartedly and without regret is to live joyfully. Let's live today to the full, jam-packed, letting the hours and minutes take care of themselves, whilst we create happiness for others in both the immediate and long-term. It is my sincerest wish that you are able to experience this feeling of joy in living for today.

November 27th

> "Throughout history, it has been the inaction of those who could have acted; the indifference of those who should have known better; the silence of the voice of justice when it mattered most; that has made it possible for evil to triumph"

Haile Selassie

With a rise of open racism and neo-nazism it is important that we speak out against those who espouse hatred, either in person or online, when we see it. This concerted effort from each of us will help us continue to live in the tolerant and inclusive society we value so highly. In addition, we can model in our own behaviour, tolerance, acceptance and compassion, so that others see this as the norm. Let's not wait for others to change, but instead continue to live positively as we are, where we are.

November 28th

"If the stars should appear but one night every thousand years how man would marvel and stare"

Ralph Waldo Emerson

Emerson is alluding to the significance of gratitude through this beautiful analogy. If all that we have in our lives was only given to us occasionally we really would appreciate it. Even though it is so much better to have all these great things each day, like drinking water, electricity, the internet, connections we have with others etc., having these things means we can take them for granted. This is natural, but can lead to us finding unhappiness in what we don't have, or what others have, rather than happiness in that which we do. One of the key components of true happiness, that comes up, study after study is gratitude. Let us not compare ourselves with others, and instead build on the precious foundation of our lives, where we stand.

November 29th

"When I was a child, life felt so slow because all I wanted to do was get into show business. Each day seemed like a year, but when you get older, years pass like minutes. I wish there was a tape recorder where we could just slow our lives down"

Bruce Forsyth

Let's not live our lives as if we are living our last day. But let's please live our lives in the full knowledge that we won't get this particular day back. May we create value for ourselves and others today, with the knowledge that we take with us, all of these positive causes into a future self that we create. Today's actions are what we will reflect back on. No day will ever present itself in the same way again with the exact same opportunities again. Let's embrace what we can do today and begin to change our situation one step at a time.

November 30th

"The essence of optimism is that it takes no account of the present, but it is a source of inspiration, of vitality and hope where others have resigned; it enables a man to hold his head high, to claim the future for himself and not to abandon it to his enemy"

Dietrich Bonhoeffer

Optimism is not blind. It is to be awakened to possibility, and possibility is truth; possibility that we will grow in strength, and begin to put every fibre of our being into the direction of changing our situation and creating value within it. True optimism is to be open to change in a world in which every single particle is impermanent by its very nature. Let's be open to change today.

December 1st

"It is during our darkest moments that we must focus to see the light"

Aristotle

Aristotle would have noted that, when fully functional, the eyes have the capacity to adjust to light conditions. We know that the adjustment of our pupils makes a significant difference and in a dark room we begin to see more and more. Our tendency when surrounded by the darkness of our problems is to have huge difficulty in adjusting our resilience level so that we begin to see a way through. So often we instead become one with the negativity that surrounds us and become so consumed by it that we are unable to take action. Before we are consumed by darkness, we should let our mind's eye adjust to the fact that the more difficult the problem we have, the more clear and determined we can be in our response. I hope we are able to adjust to any problems we are currently facing so that we can find a positive course of action to create some value for ourselves or others.

December 2nd

"Let yourself be silently drawn by the strange pull of what you really love. It will not lead you astray"

Jalal ad-Din Muhammad Rumi

Sometimes in life we get lost, thinking that our current situation and circumstances are holding us back from something. Unless our situation is harmful, it seems that it is important to bring what we really love into our life one step at a time so that our life is big enough to embrace it. Perhaps it is music, caring for others, visiting certain places, a love of animals, or a care or compassion for an interest group that means a lot to us. Whatever it is that we would like to move in the direction towards, may we let our intuition guide us and send us slowly but surely towards incorporating our love into our life, so we can continue to become a happier truer version of who we wish to be.

"No one is born hating another person because of the color of his skin or his background or his religion"

Nelson Mandela

We must never forget that we are born with a capacity to love, not hate. We must never forget that if we were to walk from hospital to hospital, from country to country, and see the newborns in any land we can imagine, we would know automatically how special each and every child is, beyond, nationality, ethnicity, gender, disability or not, the clearest thing of all, if how special life is from the get go. We must therefore have a deep respect for all, beyond behaviour and action, a deep respect of who they were or could be, and very importantly, a deep respect for ourselves too.

December 4th

"The desire to reach for the stars is ambitious. The desire to reach hearts is wise"

Maya Angelou

First reach to your own heart. Beyond the fear, worry, concern, guilt and any negativity lies compassion. In Buddhism this is referred to as your 'natural mind', 'true self' or 'greater self'. In psychology, Jung's collective consciousness comes close to expressing that which connects us to each other. I hope you get to understand the pure 'you' below all the day-to-day thoughts, feelings and concerns. Understanding and connecting with your essential selves you can first use it to enrich your own life and then reach out to others with compassion, so they can access their true self too and unlock their potential.

December 5th

"Out of suffering have emerged the strongest souls; the most massive characters are seared with scars"

Khalil Gibran

Throughout history many key figures whose names have been immortalised through their actions and their attitudes to life, had to overcome great obstacles and suffering. It is my sincere belief that they achieved a higher state of happiness from overcoming suffering than had they not experienced difficulties at all. If you are continuing despite great suffering, then your courage in doing so will eventually turn into a hue of happiness, when the winter of your suffering turns into the spring of triumph over it.

December 6th

"Believe in yourself! Have faith in your abilities! Without a humble but reasonable confidence in your own powers you cannot be successful or happy"

Norman Vincent Peale

Believing in yourself is far more about the future tense than the present or past. Believe in who you can become, believe in how much of a difference you could make to the happiness of the lives of others around you. Believe in how much you can dig deep to persevere with your current difficulties until you are through them. Believing in your capacity to face what the future will bring, gives you a fighting chance at winning in the present too.

December 7th

"In every walk with nature one receives far more than he seeks"

John Muir

More often than not, I find that thinking does not allow me to process or understand a course of action if my mind is troubled or unsure what to do. Instead I find that what I call "unthinking" or "processing activities", help clarify my mind so that I can perceive, rather than conceive, my next course of action. A walk in nature with an open mind and open heart is one of the best activities of non-thinking we can do to clear the mind, should we let go of our preconceptions and concerns during the walk itself to allow wisdom in. I hope you get to experience the nourishment that nature can give today.

December 8th

"I have just three things to teach: simplicity, patience, compassion. These three are your greatest treasures"

Lao Tzu

May we develop great compassion for others each day and may we begin to understand how special others are, and in turn how special we must be too.

December 9th

"Character cannot be developed in ease and quiet. Only through experience of trial and suffering can the soul be strengthened, ambition inspired, and success achieved"

Helen Keller

From time to time, I see the name of Keller crop up. She is the incredible human rights activist who was the first deaf-blind person to get a bachelor of honours degree. Her story is of incredible growth and development of character, through painful suffering. As you face difficulties, please know that in facing them you grow as a person. With support of her incredible teacher Anne Sullivan, Keller went on to become one of the most inspirational people to have lived in the 20th century.

December 10th

"Faith is taking the first step even when you can't see the whole staircase"

Martin Luther King Jr.

When times are difficult, the first step has to be one of faith, faith at a time when one does not know whether one will be able to turn things around. That step, when we look back, is an incredibly vital one. It is one of courage when all courage is gone, one of strength when one feels weak, and one of determination when our reserves are drained. This faith in oneself at this vital time is what makes an ordinary person a genuine hero.

December 11th

"We first make our habits, and then our habits make us"

John Dryden

The argument of this quote has been confirmed by neuroscience and psychology; we must always remember that we actively change our feelings and perceptions towards events and circumstances. This creating of new neural pathways is called neuronal plasticity. It takes time, but always work towards the idea of gradual change through facing your challenges again and again until you win. Please don't assume that these changes only take place in childhood. We are constantly making these changes in the brain. I hope this gives us hope and makes us feel like we are protagonists in this process.

December 12th

"When we seek to discover the best in others, we somehow bring out the best in ourselves"

William Arthur Ward

To seek to see the best in people is to seek to understand why they, like us, have faults. To concentrate on appreciating our own good qualities – and the things that make them human too allows us to connect. We all have differences but the more we hone in on what we possess in common, the more we open a space for dialogue – dialogue which expands our own life, every time we engage in it.

December 13th

"Your conscious brain cannot multitask. If I'm speaking to you and checking my...[phone] at the same time, I'm doing neither. This is why our society is frazzled; this misconception that we can consciously do more than one thing at a time effectively"

Deepak Chopra

Two important implications emerge from neuroscience: one, to live mindful of the moment we must focus on that which we are doing without analysis of past or present, and two, sometimes our intellect only takes us so far in addressing a problem we face; we need a process of stepping back (of non-thinking) to feel what is right by intuition too. If there is a moment today when you can just let go of your worries and be, please embrace and remember that feeling, to slowly begin to feel the way through.

December 14th

"Out beyond ideas of wrongdoing and rightdoing there is a field. I'll meet you there"

Jalal Ad-Din Muhammad Rumi

The beauty of a pure self beyond our worries, concerns, thoughts and judgements, is that we all possess this. That we all possess this inner ability to hold back our judgement and be. Let's engage with each other, with an open heart, and ever be open to ourselves too, by picking ourselves up with the kindness of a friend, on our life long journey of personal growth.

December 15th

> "Universality is a symbiotic order in which humanity, nature, and the cosmos coexist, and microcosm and macrocosm are fused.... the idea of symbiosis is conveyed by the idea of 'dependent origination.' Whether in human society or in the realm of nature, nothing exists in isolation; all phenomena are mutually supportive and related, forming a living cosmos. Once this is understood, then we can establish the proper role of reason"

Daisaku Ikeda

According to Buddhist thought we are interconnected to every other phenomenon and thus every other person too. That is why in Buddhism there is just as much wisdom found from within, as there is in books. For wisdom is an awareness as much as it is knowledge. Let's be aware today. Aware that we matter, aware that if we relax into our day and take actions that consider others, we are already living a life of sincerity and authenticity.

December 16th

"Mistakes are always forgivable, if one has the courage to admit them"

Bruce Lee

Mistakes are always going to have bad connotations when we make them, but we can choose them to have good consequences too. When we miss the mark and do wrong, by ourselves or with someone else, it is so important for our growth and happiness that we admit mistakes, and quickly use the problem as fuel in the fire for wanting to learn from them and grow, turning negative decisions or actions into a means for growth. By harbouring guilt we regress, but by harbouring instead a desire to really change that area of our lives, we genuinely revolutionise who we are: our future self. Let's harbour this positive desire today.

December 17th

"Perseverance is the hard work you do after you get tired of doing the hard work you already did"

Newt Gingrich

One day at a time may also be interpreted as what we can do to change things, from this moment on. It is to say, however hard things are, and have been, keep going. It is to say, keep moving on, moving forward, however slowly, however difficult it may be, in the direction of growth, of challenge, of creating the value within the situation, whatever that may be. Let's preserve today, and build on all our efforts to date, growing as we move our situation forward day by day.

December 18th

"We've been all the way to the moon and back, but have trouble in crossing the street to meet our new neighbour. We have built more computers to hold more information... than ever, but have less real communication"

The Dalai Lama

Today, let's get back to simplifying our lives, through treasuring the person in front of us. Listening first to understand, giving words of encouragement when such words are needed, and when times are good, lets share in what we have with a sense of gratitude and strength. May we reach out for such support if times are tough, and link up with the friends and loved ones who we can trust to nourish our lives in difficult times.

December 19th

"We are made wise not by the recollection of our past, but by the responsibility for our future."

George Bernard Shaw

May today be a day of strength, where we realise that being responsible for our lives is not a burden to share, but an exciting prospect of growth and change. There will be hardships on the way as a matter of course, but our role as the protagonist on our journey means each and every day we can grow, from where we are, step by step, action by action.

December 20th

"He who wishes to secure the good of others has already secured his own"

Confucius

If some of the actions we take today are based on the intention of enhancing the happiness of those around us, studies show that this will have a positive effect on our own mental wellbeing, even if it does make things a little busier. It is at the end of each day that we experience a sense of fulfilment from being there for others, when they need us too, and when we look back over a longer period of time we realise how much of a contribution we can have to the lives of each other. Let's keep an eye on opportunities to help others today to overcome problems by giving them perhaps the greatest gift of all, encouragement and support, because this will come back to us.

December 21st

"It's very important that we re-learn the art of resting and relaxing. Not only does it help prevent the onset of many illnesses that develop through chronic tension and worrying; it allows us to clear our minds, focus, and find creative solutions to problems"

Thich Nhat Hanh

Resting and relaxing are key examples of self-care and self-respect. If we are to learn to love ourselves fully, to show ourselves the compassion we deserve, we must listen to the physiological cues our bodies give us to signal that we need to take a break, rest or refresh. In the hectic day-to-day experience of working, parenting, caring for others, or ourselves this time can be so hard to come by. Nonetheless, striving for time to ourselves, however small, can be the most important act over time to improve our well-being and feelings of self-worth. I hope there is some time, however small, for you to slow down and recharge today.

December 22nd

"Hope is the thing with feathers that perches in the soul – and sings the tunes without the words – and never stops at all"

Emily Dickinson

In Dickinson's poem, from which the above extract is taken, the line "perches in the soul" is particularly pertinent for me because in my practice everything is either latent or manifest, myo or ho; it's two sides of the same coin. For example your anger that seems to disappear out of existence, quickly returns back when you stub your toe. Using this analogy, when hope is sometimes completely lost, please know that it lies latent waiting for the right conditions. I believe showing great courage in the face of adversity is what shines enough light for hope to sing its tune once again, so that one can struggle on with renewed determination.

December 23rd

"The truth is: belonging starts with self-acceptance. Your level of belonging, in fact, can never be greater than your level of self-acceptance, because believing that you're enough is what gives you the courage to be authentic, vulnerable and imperfect"

Brene Brown

Brown is right: if we want to be totally free to become who we want to be – our happier, braver and more considerate self – we paradoxically have to learn to accept ourselves as we are right now; with our strengths and flaws. For when we realise how being human (i.e. having flaws) is the most natural thing in the world, working with these flaws is an exciting challenge rather than a desperate fight against imperfection.

December 24th

"Christmas... is not an external event at all, but a piece of one's home that one carries in one's heart"

Freya Stark

Remember as we approach the new year and there's talk of resolutions that whilst they can be seen as positive, like "I am going to eat healthier" (he says), it is important we build who we are each and every day, always looking forward, never dwelling on the negatives of what we have said, done or what we want to change; that leads to guilt. What we instead need is the optimism that comes with change, and the determination to pick ourselves up the many times we fail, to make it, because in not giving up on any of our problems, we win the biggest victory in our lives. In not giving up on what we want to make a reality, we win, even if things do not turn out as we ourselves have planned, because in not giving up in the midst of difficulty we become who we truly want to be.

December 25th

"For what shall it profit a man, if he gains the whole world, and suffers the loss of his soul?"

Jesus Christ

In this quote, Jesus is imploring his disciples to stay absolutely true to their faith, even at the cost of their lives. He states that the alternative is to stay alive denying their beliefs, but deny their soul eternity in the process. An atheist interpretation could be this: let's not lay down our principles, trading them for the treasures of fame, status and glory, and then have to look back in our advanced years, when these things wane, with regret and low self-esteem for trading our principles for gold. If we achieve our goals and aspirations that's great, but let's do it in a way that gives us pride in ourselves and creates value for those around us in the process.

December 26th

"He who has not Christmas in his heart will never find it under a tree"

Roy L. Smith

Let's embrace our love of each other, at the deepest level this Christmas. Let's work towards forgiveness for what has been, and be open to that yet to come, continuing to strengthen our connections with those around us, and continuing to fight to open our hearts to who we wish to be.

December 27th

"A healthy attitude is contagious but don't wait to catch it from others. Be a carrier"

Tom Stoppard

This is no easy feat for us, but nonetheless a healthy attitude means being forward-thinking, not dwelling on mistakes or misfortune, but looking for ways to create happiness for oneself and others from this moment on – for a brighter future. This healthy attitude is taking a moment to think what we can do, what is possible. If we can take forward this attitude into our day, then people will see our smile and may just think, 'yes I am not powerless, I can create value too'.

December 28th

"I long to accomplish a great and noble task; but it is my chief duty to accomplish small tasks as if they were great and noble"

Helen Keller

Helen Keller is just one of many scholars who points to proficiency in the smaller things we do. To really live in this way today, to strive to do so, is to appreciate that even the small things we do make a difference to our lives, and the lives others. If we can consistently apply our efforts in this way to the tasks in front of us, even if these smaller tasks seem somewhat unimportant at the time, we will as a matter of habit spend more time in the present, growing to face the ever more demanding moments that life asks of us.

December 29th

"Youth means to cherish hope; it is a time of development. Youth means to challenge oneself; it is a time of construction. Youth means to fight for justice; it is a time of action"

Daisaku Ikeda

Mr Ikeda, who is 93 at the time of print, continues to tirelessly stand up to create a peaceful world, through his annaul work on a UN peace proposal, his continuing authorship, his dialogues with leaders in numerous political and academic fields, and his encouragement of those around him. Youth is different from aging; youth is spirit! One of my friends, in his 60s, has the most youthful spirit of anyone I know, thus in many ways he is the youngest person I know. Let's continue to strive and develop in all that we do, and continue to contribute to the growth of ourselves and others in a way that maintains our inner youthful spirit.

December 30th

"The great aim of education is not knowledge but action"

Herbert Spencer

May the education that life itself has given us so far, the ups, the downs, the suffering, the joy, shape who we are today. May our every experience and our every knowledge, enhance our ability to respond to others because of the empathy, reasoning and compassion we have developed through everything that has happened to us to date. May we be able to use that which we have overcome in our lives to date to give us the confidence to take positive action for ourselves and others around us today.

December 31st

> "I don't want to be the same person all my life. I want to be growing, I want to be expanding. I want to be changing….animate things change, inanimate things don't change. Dead things don't change. And the heart should be alive, it should be changing, it should be moving, it should be growing, its knowledge should be expanding"

Hamza Yusef

What beauty there is in this quote as we approach the new year, with our former selves behind us and look to the future selves we are yet to become. Let's not be afraid of what this coming year will bring, let's face it with an open heart and a readiness to grow, come what may.